ON HAMLET

SALVADOR DE MADARIAGA

ON
HAMLET

LONDON
HOLLIS & CARTER
1948

PRINTED IN GREAT BRITAIN BY TAPP AND TOOTHILL LTD. LEEDS AND LONDON
FOR HOLLIS AND CARTER LTD. 25 ASHLEY PLACE, LONDON S.W.1

First published in 1948

To
My Daughters
Nieves and Isabel
I dedicate this offering
to the poet their mother's
country has given to the world

CONTENTS

INTRODUCTION

CHAPTER I
HAMLET'S CHARACTER

CHAPTER II
HAMLET AND OPHELIA :
ENIGMAS AND THEIR KEY

CHAPTER III
HAMLET AND OPHELIA :
SHAKESPEARE'S OWN WORDS

CONTENTS—*continued*

CHAPTER IV
THE QUEEN AND THE KING

CHAPTER V
THE INNER TRAGEDY

CHAPTER VI
THE POET AND THE PLAY

BIBLIOGRAPHY

INTRODUCTION

TO be a constant reader of *Hamlet*, and to hold it as one of the few great masterpieces of the European spirit, is no claim to write on it; to have attempted a translation of it into Spanish verse may, however, be considered by the more generous sort fit credentials for admission into and even for a modest share in the permanent debate on the great tragedy and its meaning. For a translator must re-trace every mental step of the author, without skipping a single shade of meaning; and so may come into closer familiarity with the intentions of the master-mind than even the national critic—granted, of course, his own power to do so. Let this consideration be remembered before I am condemned for venturing to rush in where so many angels and ministers of literary grace have dared tread before me. The list is now long in which names as great as Coleridge and Bradley shine with a light so dazzling. "On a honte d'écrire des vers quand on en lit de pareils" —said Voltaire in self-disgust, reading a page of Racine. It is with feelings akin to this shame that I venture on my present task.

The more so as *Hamlet* is the masterpiece of an English genius, a genius that is foreign, in this case, to his would-be interpreter. One who has only too often had occasion to observe how the keenest and even the most creative minds, foreign to Spain, are apt to fall into the bog of incomprehension when trying to interpret Calderon or Cervantes, can not be unaware of the fact that a similar fate may well be in store for him in an attempt to present his own *Hamlet* to the people in whose midst it was born. There are, however, some ways in which a Spaniard may claim to be less foreign to Shakespeare than most other men, leaving of course aside his own kith and kin. It is not in vain that Shakespeare shone in the European firmament when the sun never set on the Spanish domains. The era of Shakespeare is the era of Spain.

Now nations reach the apex of their power when the genius of the time is in harmony with their own genius; when in other words the age acts as a sounding board for their own peculiar note. The sixteenth and seventeenth centuries were the Spanish era because then the subject of the world's debate was man on a background of absolute values—God, evil, death, love, free arbiter and predestination; all pre-eminently Spanish themes. The eighteenth century was French because by then the world's debate had shifted from the spirit to the mind, from inspiration and revelation to enquiry, from synthesis to analysis, and from religion to politics. The nineteenth century was English because by then politics had grown so thin that one could see the economic bones through the ideological skin, and the once religious or theological ethics had become secularised into social morality. And we are now entering a new era in which social mechanics or behaviourism threatens to oust social morality, an era therefore which will be the century of the U.S. or the U.S.S.R. as the case may be.

If this be true, Spaniards should be particularly apt to appreciate the spirit of the sixteenth century; for in that century what came to the surface in any one nation was that which in that nation was most in harmony with Spain. Shakespeare in particular looks upon the world with the serene eyes of an artist, indifferent to all teaching, impartial between good and evil, i.e., with that mood of the man of passion I have analysed elsewhere, as typical of the man of Spain. I have there shown that the natural attitude of the "pathic" man, of whom the Spaniard is the prototype, is that of the spectator (the Englishman, a man of action being the protagonist; the Frenchman, a man of thought, the critic). Now, in his deepest sense, Shakespeare is *a spectator of genius*. Any explanation of his works and characters which overlooks this fact, and therefore attributes to him a purpose, a bias, a tendency, should be suspected as likely to lead to error. Shakespeare just looks, sees and re-creates what is there.

The purely fortuitous fact that such is the specific natural attitude of the Spaniard is therefore my second excuse for venturing to write on *Hamlet*. In the course of my translation I had often to consult the many and admirable essays written by English and American critics on the play and its characters; and, to be sure, met more than once with this central thought of all Shakesperean criticism set down as clearly as could be wished, i.e. that Shakespeare is unbiased, all-embracing, "above the strife". But it soon became evident to me that the principle, once stated and proclaimed, was apt to be forgotten when it might have been invaluable to explain a character or to analyze a situation. It is, of course, utterly impossible even to attempt a criticism of *Hamlet's* critics; for our present purpose, however, it is necessary to point out that, after having been made to indulge in an orgy of character interpretation, which naively identified Shakespeare's characters with human beings, we are now led too far in the opposite direction, and bidden to be content with a Shakespeare who *depicted* characters without bothering as to their motivations. The greatest poet, the keenest observer of human nature is thus declared to have taken no interest in the motives which made his characters act as they did. This conclusion, convenient though it be for the critics whom Shakespeare's subtlety—and occasional lapses into carelessness—baffles, must be brushed aside as irrelevant. The principle that shall rule over all our enquiries is that Shakespeare knew what he was doing—even if, at times, he fell below his own, or our standards of craftsmanship.

Here is the *Gioconda*. Of course, it would be childish to describe her as an actual woman; and those critics who tell us all about Hamlet's youth or how Ophelia may have learnt those unseemly songs from her wicked nurse, do fall into that mistake. But are we to follow the "historical" critics whose theory amounts to solemnly warning us that the *Gioconda* is just a piece of cloth covered with oil and pigment so as to *depict* a woman? No more but so?—as

Ophelia would ask. Was then Leonardo so indifferent to the inner Mona Lisa that he paid no attention to coordinating eyes and lips, cheeks and forehead into a spiritual and psychological perspective? Of course we know that out of words and lines, images and situations, Shakespeare was but cleverly contriving an illusion. But the force, the depth and the creative quality behind this illusion come from the fact that it is conceived from the intuition of a coherent *psyche* living behind its seemingly incoherent gestures and motions—that, in Shakespeare's own words, though "infinite in faculty, in form and moving", it is "express and admirable in action".[1]

[1] It s significant that such a prominent exponent of the historical school as Dr. Stoll discusses little else but Hamlet's *character* which otherwise he apparently denies. "But what of our hero?"— he asks at the end of an utterly unconvincing refusal to see any procrastination in Hamlet—"In ridding him (whom? what *person*?) of his fault have we also robbed him of his charm? If not weak and erring, he is still unfortunate enough, unhappy enough to be tragic". *Stoll-H*, p. 68. See also "By his tone and bearing, likewise, and a conduct that is (if we be not cavilling) irreproachable, and a reputation that is stainless, is Hamlet to be judged".—*Stoll A*, p. 104.

CHAPTER I

HAMLET'S CHARACTER

§ 1: *In Search of a Character for the Chief Character.*

Most of the difficulties we encounter in understanding *Hamlet* come from a disharmony between the taste of present day Britain and that of Shakespearean England. In Shakespeare's days, England was still uninhibited; and puritanism—the making of her greatness-in-action—had not yet blasted her greatness-in-art. Three great English names mark the three degrees whereby spiritual-aesthetic England steps down to puritan and later to social-political Britain: Shakespeare - Milton - Wordsworth. Some of Milton's poetical gifts, such as his musical power; some of his human traits such as the sensuousness which, though often hidden and repressed, graces his verse; and even some of his defects, such as his passionate hatreds and his love of invective, make one wonder whether, had such a genius been born one century earlier, England and the world would not have seen a rival of Shakespeare—an almost incredible event. As for Wordsworth, since he wrote himself "I wish either to be considered as a teacher, or as nothing", there is nothing we can do to save him. This sentence measures not only the difference between Wordsworth and Shakespeare (who, we may be sure, lived in holy horror of all teaching), but the distance—downwards in aesthetic terms, upwards in political terms—England had travelled from Shakespeare to Wordsworth. The Britain of Wordsworth, prim and respectable, had to adapt Shakespeare to her tastes and ways. Hamlet the Elizabethan had to be modernised. And to begin with he had to shave. For Hamlet was bearded like Drake and not clean shaven like Mr. Winston Churchill.

1

Who calls me villain, breaks my pate across,
Plucks off my beard and blows it in my face,

II.2. 575-6.

Then, he had to take off his hat indoors; for Hamlet, indoors, like all Elizabethans, kept his hat on his head; a custom so well established that Ophelia was ever "so affrighted" on seeing him come before her into her closet "No hat upon his head". Indeed that hat became so much of a nuisance to us moderns, that Hamlet usually wears none in our day even when travelling, even when coming out to meet the Ghost on the castle platform when, hatless to suit us, he exclaims: "The air bites shrewdly, it is very cold". *Hamlet* should be staged in Elizabethan style; all men wearing hats in and out of doors; save when the King is present, when all but Hamlet and Polonius (possibly Laertes also) should take off their hats and don them again as the King leaves. Hamlet should be hatless if and when he must give the impression of being in one of his fits of 'sore distraction'. Hamlet says to Osric: "Put your bonnet to his right use, 'tis for the head".

These, it may be argued, are but trifling infidelities. And so, up to a point, they are. But they surely must conceal some substantial import or else we should not insist so much on inflicting them on *Hamlet*. At any rate, they suggest the process of deformation and adaptation which the character has undergone. The beard, the hat and feathers, are all outward signs of a barbarous (if brilliant) age; they have to be sacrificed, not in themselves, but because we must first get rid of these outward signs before we come to alter the inner man. It is Hamlet himself, his person and spirit, we want to assimilate to our century. He, the Elizabethan, the volcano of manly energies, ever in spontaneous eruption, must be turned into a grassy hill and become genteel. Hamlet, the man born in an era of no gentleness whatever, must become a gentleman.

And, to begin with, he must be likeable: everybody, that is, must be able to like him, beginning with Shakespeare.

2

An eminent modern critic is in fact certain that Hamlet was a "hero whom Shakespeare loved above all other creatures of his brain";[1] though to an objective reader what is certain is that, in so far as Shakespeare was capable of love—a fascinating topic in itself—he loved Claudius and Polonius, indeed Osric, exactly as much as he did Hamlet.

This and many similar utterances combine the two attitudes which together are bound to distort out of recognition the true intention and meaning of Shakespeare: on the one hand, the poet, we are told, loved Hamlet "above all other creatures of his brain," i.e. Shakespeare takes sides; on the other, Hamlet is *the* hero, he is the one who is right; he is 'my' favourite in this play, and I am meant to 'sympathise' with him in a special way, i.e. to take sides in the play and be of his 'party'. Neither of these assumptions, I submit, is correct. It is true that Shakespeare asks us to sympathize with Hamlet, but his greatness lies precisely in that he asks us to sympathize with every single man and woman in the play, not excluding the clown in the churchyard. It is impossible fully to understand Shakespeare unless this point is realised—he was absolutely impartial and created "heroes" and "criminals" for the stage with as much serenity as the Spirit creates them for the world. For, in fact, neither Shakespeare nor the Spirit create heroes or criminals; since "nothing is either good or bad but thinking makes it so". Shakespeare's creatures are alive precisely because they evade all labels.

Much of what has been written on Hamlet, is biased in his favour. The critic, we feel, does not face the full impact of the facts, drawing then the conclusions which inevitably follow as to the character; he starts determined to "explain", and, if need be, to "explain away" all the facts more or less awkward for Hamlet the hero, Hamlet the gentleman, Hamlet the sweet, for that "peculiar beauty and nobility of his nature"[2] which goes without saying. Owing to this

[1] D.W., p. 44.

[2] Bradley, p. 138.

defective 'stance' of their affections, even acute observers are apt to describe the events in *Hamlet* in a manner which bears little relation to the actual facts of the play.

This bias may well account for the peculiar incoherence which still attaches to Hamlet. True, there are at least two other causes for it. The first is the complex origin of the play and of his protagonist. Since the date of *Hamlet's* composition is now more in doubt than ever, the only elements that can be taken for certain as having entered in its composition are the *Historia Danica* of Saxo Grammaticus and the *Histoires Tragiques* of Belleforest. The hypothetical and perhaps legendary *Hamlet-before-Hamlet* may well turn out to be *Hamlet* itself; and *The Spanish Tragedy* may well never have influenced Shakespeare at all.[1] But even when reduced to the Danish story in its two versions, Latin and French, Hamlet comes to Shakespeare endowed with a certain incoherence, due in part to his assumed folly. And if, as is still generally held to be the case, other plays influenced Shakespeare, the original incoherence would be greater still.

But, surely, it is hardly historical to imagine that a spirit of the creative vigour of Shakespeare would succumb under the weight and variety of the materials he found in the lumber room of his workshop and fail to erect his own construction. Whatever the "hang-over" here and there, Shakespeare had a clear and consistent notion of his characters—and, above all, of Hamlet, the protagonist of his play. Now, so far, Hamlet's many facets and moods have been admirably described by a score of critics and analysts; but no attempt seems to have been made to endow the explorer of that labyrinth which is his soul with an Ariadne's thread—or in other words, his character with a psychological spine.

This spine would appear to be the more indispensable because of that "antic disposition", an apt illustration to what has just been set down as to the relations between the historical raw material and the use a great artist can make

[1] Cf. Cairncross.

of it. The character of Hamlet is so closely intertwined with madness by tradition that the very name of Hamlet seems to convey the fact. Hamlet comes from Amleth; which comes from Amlóði; which comes from Aml-ód, i.e. Onela the mad.[1] The primitive Hamlet was mad in an uncouth, indeed brutish way; and he showed it in particular by his lack of manners and his slovenly and even dirty ways. Shakespeare is the heir of this tradition, and whatever "madness" we witness in the play is the outcome of his genius at work on the traditional raw material. There is a general and pre-existent madness in Hamlet which comes from tradition, and a special and concrete "madness", localised north-north-west which is moulded by Shakespeare. When Hamlet is unbalanced by the vision of the Ghost and the heavy task this visitation lays on his shoulders he passes from his general predisposition to madness, traditionally associated with his character, to the special north-north-west madness of what now becomes an *idée fixe* for him; and on top of it all, he puts on a mask of madness to move at greater freedom during the hard days he guesses ahead. Hamlet is, therefore, a traditionally mad man, maddened by the meeting with the Ghost and disguised as a madman.

Yet, here, a caution. Far too much is made in criticism of Hamlet's madness and melancholy. He himself warns us he is only mad in craft. And the fact is that while there is in him a good deal of 'antics' there is but little melancholy and no madness whatever when these two words are taken in their concrete medical terms. An artist can use a madman here and there in his composition; he can not build a great work on a madman as his central theme. (No. Don Quixote is not an argument against this statement, for he also was only "mad" in a north-north-west of his own. He knew full well how not to test his cardboard vizor.) The use and abuse of 'melancholy' to explain now the South wind in the hawk-and-handsaw phrase, now Hamlet's coarseness to-

[1] The Literary History of Hamlet (ch. II, p. 52-55), by Kemp Malone, Ph.D., Heidelberg, 1923.

wards Ophelia, and so nearly every passage in the play, has led to too much confusion and waste of time. Let it be understood that Hamlet's "madness" is a very much exaggerated feature, and that he really was only mad in craft.

For a poet of Shakespeare's resource, the staging of such a complex character was not merely easy; it was an enjoyable task; for it enabled him to indulge at will in his riotous intellectual creativeness. In feigning madness Hamlet gives marvellous freedom not only to himself but to his creator. This is one of the causes of that feeling of space which *Hamlet* leaves in both reader and spectator. Hamlet wanders about in the vast world of thought, or rather flies about in its air, for at no point does he give that sense of "crawling" which he denounces in one of his gloomy moods.

But, conversely, the freer, indeed the more incoherent his words and gestures, the more coherent his actual deeds and inner attitudes must be if we are to keep an interest in the tragedy. "Whatever weakness we may be expected to find in Hamlet's character,"—writes a modern expert[1]—"however severely Shakespeare judges him and asks us to judge him also, it is vital to his purpose that we should retain our interest in him and admiration for him right up to the end. Rob us of our respect for the hero and Hamlet ceases to be a tragedy." May I differ again? Admiration for the hero is by no means necessary for the tragedy—nor even respect. What is necessary is coherence in the character. The words quoted above are applied to Hamlet's "unexplained behaviour" to Ophelia; i.e. the critic starts from the need to respect and admire Hamlet lest the tragedy disappears; and goes on to "explain" why he treats Ophelia—how? in a way he, by now, can no longer see with unbiased eyes. The true method is the reverse. We first watch Hamlet "behaving" towards Ophelia, and then draw our conclusions as to what kind of a person Hamlet was. Respect and admiration, like the devil, will take the hindmost.

[1] D.W., p. 102.

Ophelia's troubles will be examined anon. For the present we must endeavour to find the *key to unity* in Hamlet's character. We must be certain that Shakespeare could not have felt so free to present his protagonist under so many lights, had he not possessed a guide, a principle to endow his character with the inner unity his outward pranks and adventures were bound to lack.

§ 2. *Hamlet and Don Quixote.*

In order to discover this key, let us take a round-about way; let us compare Hamlet and Don Quixote. Here is a parallel between these two great Europeans, borrowed from another study on the subject.

Hamlet and Don Quixote provide one of the most fascinating parallels in literature: possibly because the two poets who created them were contemporaries and, unknown to each other, spoke the same idiom. It would be childish to limit either of these two great characters to that particular aspect which lends itself to be lit up by the light that emanates from the other. But, with this reservation, the parallel between Hamlet and Don Quixote is one of the clearest ways of approach not only to the knowledge of either of them, but also to the study of Europe and her permanent problems.

At the outset we must get rid of a popular though, of course, by no means scholarly misconception about Hamlet. He is not irresolute. Nothing more unlike Hamlet than the effeminate fastidiousness with which he is at times represented. He is resolute to a fault, indeed to two faults: impulsiveness and brutality. The man who could hoist Rosencrantz and Guildenstern with their own petard, or coldly drag Polonius' body out of the room in which he had killed him, was not squeamish, fastidious or irresolute. But, of course, misconceptions do not arise out of nothing. Hamlet is at times believed to be irresolute because the whole play is woven of his hesitations on the threshold of the task the Ghost has set before him. It is, however, evident that

Hamlet, to borrow his own image, is only irresolute north-north-west. When the Ghost beckons him away from his companions, he is resolute; when the Ghost points to King Claudius as a man to be slain, he hesitates.

He hesitates, but he does not refuse. He is, as the pregnant English saying goes, in two minds about it. And the question arises: whence the two minds? It is the crucial question to the interpretation of Hamlet. The answer to this question will reveal the essentially European and ever modern character of this Englishman who stalks the European Olympus clad in the garb of a Prince of Denmark.

Let us see him first in his setting, as Ophelia, in her lamentations, describes him for us.

> O, what a noble mind is here o'erthrown!
> The courtier's, soldier's, scholar's, eye, tongue, sword:
> The expectancy and rose of the fair State,
> The glass of fashion and the mould of form,
> The observed of all observers,

In these words, Ophelia reveals one of the most important factors about Hamlet. He occupies the centre of his world, the apex of his society. He is the observed of all observers and the expectancy of the State; the glass of fashion and the mould of form. Poor, unfortunate prince; he must satisfy all observers, fulfil all expectations, passively reflect all fashions and take into his soul any paste or dough in search of form! And we wonder he was unhappy!

This then is the initial position. A young, vigorous, brave, intelligent, active man (he tells his friend he has of late "forgone all custom of exercises"), a man, therefore, bound to have a mind of his own, finds himself confined within a society of closely knit traditions, ways and ideas. So far, though the tension must have been there all the time, there has been no conflict. True, Hamlet is prone to emphasise now and then that he does not respect custom *qua* custom, but only if it justifies itself in his eyes. Shakespeare took care to hint at this:

"Is it a custom?"
asks Horatio when drums and trumpets "bray out" the
King's toast, and Hamlet answers:

Ay, marry, is't.
But to my mind, though I am native here
And to the manner born, it is a custom
More honour'd in the breach than the observance.

For whom are these words meant? Certainly not for
Hamlet's interlocutors on the stage. Horatio and Marcellus
are as Danish as Hamlet, and presumably as well versed in
the customs of Denmark, though Shakespeare makes
Horatio and not Marcellus ask the question to pass it off
better on the score of his long stay in Wittenberg. In any
case that "though I am native here and to the manner born"
is a hint to the audience to the effect that Hamlet is by no
means ready to enter without protest into the part which
Ophelia tells us the State expects of him. We see thus from
the outset the nature of the conflict: the society known as the
State of Denmark is bent on moulding Hamlet to its image
and expectations, setting all its observers on him; and the
individual Hamlet asserts his right to judge for himself
when and why he will follow the dictates of the society in
the midst of which he was born.

At this stage, the Ghost appears. Why a Ghost? Because
he represents tradition, the voice of the dead who still live
and beyond death still order us about. We need not assume
that Shakespeare deliberately brings the Ghost on to the
stage because of this symbolic value; he probably did not,
and in any case, the Ghost was traditional in the plot—but
the facts of nature, not the poet, grant him this power to
represent the voice of the dead—i.e. tradition. The Ghost
orders Hamlet to avenge a crime with another crime. All
that is social in Hamlet pushes Hamlet to his deed: he
must obey his father, tradition, the Ghost, the vindictive-
ness of society whereby it protects itself against deeds which
would destroy it; in other words, against all that is rotten
in the Kingdom of Denmark. But the individual Hamlet

cannot bring himself to commit that individual crime which
is a social execution. The conflict is absolute; and the whole
play moves inexorably towards Hamlet's death.

Don Quixote is almost a perfect antithesis of all this.
While Hamlet is a young man of action, living in the centre
and on the apex of a society thickly woven with the threads
of customs, fashions, traditions and forms, Don Quixote is
an idle, indolent and dreamy man of passion, whiling away
his empty time in the empty spaces of the Manchegan
plains, unobserved, unknown, alone. Instead of the pressure
of a strong society on an unwilling individual; the void of a
rarefied, almost inexistent environment round an individual
hungry for something to happen. Instead of a peremptory
call to concrete action on the part of tradition, an action
repugnant to the man who must perform it; an unsolicited
offer of vague and general action by the Knight Errant—
note Errant that is aimless—to a society which has no use
for it. Instead of a pressure converging on the man of action
rendered passive and dreamy by the conflict; the dispersion
and dissipation of the man of passion, turned active and
executive by the lack of social pressure to absorb his inner
urge. Restlessness arises in both cases; and then, Hamlet,
the man of action thrown back upon himself by his inability
to tackle the first act he must perform if he act at all,
wanders about watching things and people, and philosophising about them; seeing in all that happens examples and
comments on his own state; while Don Quixote rides forth,
not passively meeting by the caprice of luck with churchyard clowns or Scandinavian princes, but actively seeking
adventures which he forces on nature and society when
society and nature do not give them forth. So that, while
more than once he comes to grief and falls into ridicule,
more than once also he forces his surroundings to adopt his
view of life and live for a while at least in his fantastic world.

Violence in both cases. For in that of Hamlet, the solid
soul of a strong man of action, who knows what he wants
and what he does not want, has to suffer violence from a

society determined to master and tame him; while in that of Don Quixote the idle dreamer is led by the circumambient void to sally forth in order to impress his own dream-world on the world of circumstance.

Hamlet and Don Quixote are thus at the opposite sides of the ideal answer to the central problem of all human societies: that of the balance between the individual and the community in which he lives. "The world is too much with us"—said Wordsworth; but he also spoke of those who had felt the weight of too much liberty. Hamlet would have been with him in the former mood; Don Quixote in the latter. And it is difficult to take leave of this pair of immortal Europeans without a haunting feeling that Hamlet's soliloquies are the parallel to D. Quixote's sallies. The pressure of his too, too socialised world drove the Prince's soul within, determining those spiral-like soliloquies, sallies or adventures of passion in the fields of the soul, which, ever narrower and narrower, ended in the pointed bodkin of self-slaughter; the void of his rarefied world drew the Knight out of himself to those spiral-like sallies, soliloquies of action ever wider and wider, which ended in disaster and frustration on the sterile dust of the desert. So with all of us—ever threatened with the unutterable misery of an efficient, oppressive society or with the inane and fertile agitation of the human being in a society which fails to cast itself into a living shape. Hamlet and Don Quixote stand watch on the two roads by which society and man stray from the royal road of sense—one, over which Hamlet broods, leads to tyranny through too much order; the other one, over which Don Quixote dreams, leads to anarchy through no order at all. The royal road of sense lies between the two. But . . . it must be guessed.

§ 3.   *Hamlet's Backbone.*

One point to be gathered from this parallel is that it provides a natural setting for Hamlet's "madness". His state gains clarity by being described in symmetry with that of D.

Quixote. Since the Spanish knight, alone in the empty spaces of La Mancha, lost his mental balance for lack of pressure in the social atmosphere, the Danish Prince may well have lost his because the social pressure round him was too high. It may be argued that the other characters did not find it as unbearable as all that; but there are two answers: that Hamlet was 'the observed of all observers', i.e. the recipient of the utmost pressure; and that he was more susceptible to social pressure than any other character in the play.

This exceptional susceptibility to social pressure points to the chief feature in the character. More than any one else in the play, indeed in all the Shakespearean stage, or world, Hamlet is a differentiated man. He acts, thinks, feels, not in the Danish, or the English, but in the Hamletian way. Hence his constant strife against his environment; his philosophising; and his loneliness. Modern psychology has endeavoured to explain scientifically what genius had discovered at all times: that beyond a certain degree of differentiation, the mind is unhinged and madness sets in. Strindberg and Nietzsche are two tragic examples of brilliant minds destroyed by too much divorce from the mind-of-all. It was one of Shakespeare's strokes of genius that he raised the brutish and sub-human madness of the traditional Amleth from a level below the common to that level above the common where the intellect wavers out of giddiness.

This distance which Hamlet manages to establish between himself and the world is a great dramatic asset. It contributes not a little to that feeling that in this tragedy he and he alone matters. Not even Ophelia can retain our attention for long; and her sad fate, her mad scene, her death, her burial, soon become a mere part of Hamlet's dream, mere clouds in Hamlet's sky. As soon as Hamlet is on the stage, everything and everybody becomes background. *Hamlet* is a Hamlet-centric play.

It follows that Hamlet is egocentric. And this is the key we were looking for. The only principle capable of giving an order and a coherence to the character, the only explanation for all he says and does, is that Hamlet is egocentric. This is the meaning to be attached to the famous line "for there is nothing either good or bad, but thinking (i.e. *my* thinking) makes it so". There is—he means—no objective standard. He has just said Denmark is a prison. Rosencrantz retorts: "We think not so, my Lord;" and he, at once, concedes: "Why, then 'tis none to you, for there is nothing either good or bad, but thinking makes it so: to me it is a prison".

This is the triumph of subjectivity. In these words, Hamlet defines what throughout the play he performs: good or bad are to be understood in relation to him. Hamlet is as egocentric in his standards of action as in his standards of thought. It is in so far as, and in the way in which, situations affect him that he reacts. Once this principle is recognised, the play, so much involved and so difficult, becomes crystal clear. The only reason why so many of Hamlet's actions give rise to interminable discussions and to complicated explanations is that the bias which will make of him a refined, noble, sweet, generous gentleman—no doubt with his 'weaknesses' and even his 'savagery' but a gentleman at heart—provides no definite set of co-ordinates for them. But when we realise that the centre of Hamlet's interest, thought, motive and emotion is his own self, the play becomes as clear as the solar system after Copernicus, when astronomers were able at last to drop their cycles and epicycles and refer everything in simple ellipses to the sun.

§ 4. *Rosencrantz and Guildenstern.*

Ce monsieur est un imbécile. C'est moi qui le dit; c'est lui qui le prouve. This anecdote may now be applied to our subject. We have put forward the view that Hamlet is an egocentric man, and that his actions must remain obscure until we realise that he only acts when his own interests are directly concerned. He is going to prove us right. Even nowadays, the best authorities can write that Hamlet's procrastination

"is considered his most mysterious feature".[1] But why?
Because its motives are sought where they cannot be found.
This procrastination cannot be due to an instinctive and
fastidious repugnance to killing, for Hamlet kills Polonius,
and Laertes, and in the end the King himself; and he
dispatches Rosencrantz and Guildenstern to their doom with
true alacrity. Whence then does it come?

The answer will be found by examining all these cases.
And before them all, let us look at those two lines in I.4.

> unhand me gentlemen,
> By heaven I'll make a ghost of him that lets me!

It is one of the key points in the drawing of his character.
When it comes to doing what he is determined to do, he
will not hesitate to kill even his closest friend, for Horatio
is one of the gentlemen whom he threatens sword in hand.
Hamlet's spontaneous tendencies are therefore essentially
individualistic; and, the point must be emphasised, not even
death of others, if need be, will stand in his way.

This is the Hamlet whose behaviour towards Rosencrantz and Guildenstern we are now to study. They were
his friends, and we know from his mother that he had much
talked of them and that

> two men there are not living
> To whom he more adheres.

The two young men receive from the King a commission
which, whatever the King's secret intentions may be, is
honourable. Hamlet, the King in fact tells them, is not
what he was. The cause of the change "I cannot dream of".
Therefore, I beg you

> so by your companies
> To draw him on to pleasures, and to gather
> So much as from occasion you may glean
> Whether aught to us unknown afflicts him thus
> That opened lies within our remedy.

Guildenstern's words show that the two young men
understand their work in an irreproachable way:

[1] D.W., p. lix.

Heaven make our presence and our practices
Pleasant and helpful to him.

They enter upon their new duties at a later stage in the
same scene. Cordial and light-hearted, the meeting of the
three young men leads to some fencing of wits on ambition;
for Rosencrantz and Guildenstern, who know nothing about
King Hamlet's murder, naturally assume that the trouble
with Hamlet is frustrated ambition (and so in part it is):
Hamlet, of course, parries, and as he tries to move off, his
two companions, in strict obedience to their master, the
King, say: "We'll wait upon you." This raises his suspicions.
"But, in the beaten way of friendship, what make you at
Elsinore?" They are put out. Very likely they had not
expected this alertness in a Hamlet the King had depicted

So much from th'understanding of himself.

They try to plot a concerted answer, but in the end are
honest to him; and to his direct question they return a direct
answer: "My lord, we were sent for."

This scene is typical. Bearing in mind that, for Rosencrantz and Guildenstern, the King was their legitimate
sovereign, and that for all they knew, Hamlet was at least
"queer", the two young men acquit themselves of their
delicate duties with skill and dignity. They do make mis-
takes later, and, as Guildenstern openly avows: "O my
lord, if my duty be too bold, my love is too unmannerly."
But this other scene is one in which Hamlet's whole in-
considered egotism shows itself unashamed. He is, of course,
excited by the triumph of his stratagem, the play, whereby
he has proved the Ghost right and the King a criminal;
yet this circumstance merely raises the pitch of his mood,
without in any way altering the essence of his character.
His behaviour towards Rosencrantz and Guildenstern is
rude in the extreme. "This courtesy is not of the right
breed," says Guildenstern; and when Rosencrantz points out
to him "you once did love me," his answer is: "And do
still, by these pickers and stealers." He has a case; of course
he has a case. And he puts it with unforgettable beauty and

15

truth in his apologue on the recorder. " 'Sblood, do you think I am easier to be played on than a pipe?" And one can conceive his irritation at being followed and accompanied when he would prefer to be alone. But, when all is said and pondered on his behalf, the scene remains an exhibition of complete self-centredness and of utter disregard for the feelings of others.

Matters have entered on a new phase, after the play. The King believes or choses to believe that Hamlet's madness is dangerous, and in III.3 warns Rosencrantz and Guildenstern that he intends to send them to England with Hamlet. Both deliver themselves of somewhat fulsome utterances on the importance of the King's safety; but no word is said to warrant the view that they are in the least shaken as to their loyalty and friendship for the unhappy and, as they think, 'distempered' Prince. Then Hamlet kills Polonius. Rosencrantz and Guildenstern hear the news from the King and, without a word, obey the order to go and find the body. Hamlet receives them abominably. They have done nothing to deserve being insulted as Hamlet does here and treated as sponges kept in the corner of one's jaw, and all the rest of this tirade no man with human feelings would address even to a slave. Here again, every word can be explained from the point of view of Hamlet's feelings, but only when it is agreed that for Hamlet his feelings are the one thing that matters and nothing else matters at all.

In the next scene, Rosencrantz brings Hamlet 'guarded' before the King. The Prince has committed at least manslaughter. The guard is justified. Rosencrantz's action also, even in Hamlet's eyes. After a dialogue, to be studied anon, which can hardly increase the confidence of Rosencrantz and Guildenstern in Hamlet's sanity, the King reiterates his orders for the three men to embark soon; and it is the clear intention of the author that the public should know that the King of Denmark writes to the King of England to put Hamlet to death, but that this letter is sealed and that Rosencrantz and Guildenstern know nothing about it. To this effect, Shakespeare gets rid first of the three voyagers and then lets the King think aloud and let out his secret.

Then comes the most unlikely piece of dramatic trickery in the tragedy; that pirate ship which turns up just in order to bring Hamlet back to the play and send Rosencrantz and Guildenstern on to England. We hear it all from a letter to Horatio. The pirates, of course, being "thieves of mercy", took great care to wait to attack till Hamlet had had time to have the engineer hoist with his own petard. His intention to do so escaped him in conversation with his mother.

> There's letters sealed, and my two school-fellows,
> Whom I will trust as I will adders fanged,
> They bear the mandate—they must sweep my way
> And marshal me to knavery: let it work,
> For 'tis the sport to have the enginer
> Hoist with his own petard, and't shall go hard
> But I will delve one yard below their mines,
> And blow them at the moon.

Here Hamlet reveals a mistrust of his two school-fellows which they do not deserve; but the worst of which he suspects them is of bearing the mandate to marshal him to knavery; i.e. to debar him from fulfilling his ambition by keeping him in exile. Moreover, he knows the letters are sealed.

Yet, the last line is already a warning of his intention to "blow them to the moon". *Them* can only mean Rosencrantz and Guildenstern. And sure enough, he himself imparts to Horatio how, having broken the seals, and read what his uncle had in store for him, he wrote another commission requiring the King of England to put his two school fellows to death. Why? What had they done to him? They would have been horrified had they known either about the contents of the sealed letter or about the murder of Hamlet's father. What is Hamlet's reason for committing so dastardly an action? Here it is:

> Why, man, they did make love to this employment,
> They are not near my conscience, their defeat
> Does by their own insinuation grow.

> 'Tis dangerous when the baser nature comes
> Between the pass and fell incensèd points
> Of mighty opposites   V.2.57–62.

And that is all. Unless one adds these revealing words to his mother on the same theme:

> O, 'tis most sweet
> When in one line two crafts directly meet.

These words describe the man. Hamlet was a Renaissance European who thought that all was permissible to the powerful for the sake of power, and that those who were not of 'the baser nature' need not follow the rules of the game. Shakespeare, as was his wont, has rendered this feature of his character not merely by deeds, not merely by words, but by moods. Clearer even than the cool explanation of what amounts to his murder of Rosencrantz and Guildenstern, is the flippant, frivolous way in which he relates it:

> Wilt thou know
> Th' effect of what I wrote?

he asks Horatio; and then, relishing every word of it with the gusto of a true *dilettante*, he speaks on:

> An earnest conjuration from the king,
> As England was his faithful tributary,
> As love between them like the palm might flourish,
> As peace should still her wheaten garland wear
> And stand a comma 'tween their amities,
> And many such like 'as'es' of great charge,
> That on the view and knowing of these contents,
> Without debatement further, more or less,
> He should those bearers put to sudden death,
> Not shriving-time allowed.   V.2.38–46.

Genius could go no higher to represent the utter human callousness of a brilliant wit, for whom the very detail of not allowing time for confession, a truly terrible cruelty in those days, is reserved for an effect in the story. Hamlet in this scene is happy, thoroughly happy. He has won; he has played his uncle a mighty trick; he pokes witty fun at diplomatic papers; he tells a story as no one else can; that he kills two men so to enjoy himself, is a mere detail— moreover, they were of 'the baser nature'.

In his attitude towards his two schoolfellows, Hamlet, therefore, confirms our view of him as a man predominantly interested in himself; a man, therefore, for whom the other persons, without exception, are but pawns in his game. For such a character the worst crime that can be committed by an outsider is an aggression against his own self. The savagery with which Hamlet sends Rosencrantz and Guildenstern to their doom is due to his sudden discovery that the King meant to have him put to death. This personal aggression is for Hamlet the very apex of crime. His emotion at seeing himself thus attacked seals the fate of his two schoolfellows, even though he knew them to be innocent. He would not tell them his secret—the Ghost's secret—which would almost certainly have brought them over to his party; and he made them responsible for a loyalty to the King which in the circumstances was imperative. This had been enough to create in his Machiavellian or Borgian mind the desire to blow them to the moon. The energy for the explosion came from the thrust at his body which the commission revealed when he broke the seals. At no time did he think of his two school fellows as human beings in their own right. And when, even in imagination, his skin was threatened, he took their lives.

This, we shall see, is a permanent feature in Hamlet's character. It is, therefore, important not to misread it. Hamlet does not react so quickly to threats to his skin because he fears death or pain. He is brave. His threat to make a ghost of him who 'lets', i.e. who prevents, him from following the Ghost is virile; he is the first to board that pirate ship, and though we have no word but his for it, we do not hesitate to believe him; for despite his subtleties and his "pranks" he strikes that note of frankness which always goes with courage. No. The swiftness of his reactions when attacked is not cowardice; it is egotism. It means: "you are welcome to do anything you like in the world, but you must not touch ME."

§ 5. *Polonius.*

Hamlet's behaviour towards Polonius confirms all these conclusions, and proves them to be in harmony with the deliberate intentions of the author. All good critics agree that Polonius should not be conceived as a caricature; that he is a kind of Secretary of State as well as Chamberlain, and that his intellectual powers, while just beginning to decline and soften into garrulousness, still deserve the King's trust implied in his high functions. This should be duly weighed when appraising Hamlet's relations with him— leaving for a later page the fact that Polonius is the father of Ophelia.

It is mostly as Ophelia's father that Hamlet maltreats Polonius in their first meeting (II.2), which had better therefore be treated later; but we might observe in passing that, whatever motives we are to discover for his actions and attitude, Hamlet does not spare the old man and treats him, as he does everybody, like an object; while his remark when left alone is "These tedious old fools!" There is an extenuating circumstance in this scene: Hamlet and Polonius are alone, and the old counsellor is made the Prince's sport for no one but the Prince. No humiliation is implied.

Not so at a later stage in the same scene (II.2) when Polonius breaks in to announce the arrival of the players. Here Hamlet turns Polonius into a clown for him to disport himself with before an audience. "Hark you, Guildenstern, and you too"—he says to his two schoolmates—"at each ear a hearer—that great baby you see there is not yet out of his swaddling-clouts." And a comedy follows in which Hamlet is the witty man, Polonius the victim of his wit, and Rosencrantz and Guildenstern the chorus and the audience. Worse, however, is to come. The actors arrive, and the First Player declaims his 'passionate speech'; after forty-nine lines of which, Polonius utters what the whole

20

audience is surely thinking: "This is too long." Hamlet's reaction is savage: "It shall to the barber's with your beard; prithee say on—he's for a jig or a tale of bawdry, or he sleeps—say on, come to Hecuba."

This in the presence of the actors, spoken with the utmost contempt. Even in our day it would be deemed injurious to any well-bred man's reputation; but in the days of the despised actor, so to treat the most dignified subject of the Kingdom was sheer moral cruelty of the deepest dye.[1] Can such a retort be passed over and Hamlet still be described as a courteous, noble-minded, sweet-mannered gentleman? These words reveal a callous egotist, intent on his own satisfaction to the utter disregard of anyone else's feelings. True Polonius takes it coolly, believing Hamlet is mad; and humours him soon after, following heavily on Hamlet's critical steps about 'the mobled queen'. But this in no way detracts from Hamlet's callousness, for he knows what he is doing. He knows it so well that he later says to the First Player: "Follow that lord, and look you mock him not"; for he realises he has shown them the way; yet does not want them to imitate him, since, after all they are of 'the baser nature' and not entitled to the sport of the great.

Hamlet's meeting with Polonius in III.1 must be left for a later stage in our study. But a note should be made of the passage in III.2 when in the presence of the King, the Queen, Ophelia, Rosencrantz, Guildenstern and other courtiers, the following dialogue takes place:

Polonius: I did enact Julius Caesar. I was killed i'th' Capitol. Brutus killed me.

Hamlet: It was a brute part of him to kill so capital a calf there

after which unnecessary jest, entailing an unnecessary humiliation of the old man, he coldly turns to ask, "Be the players ready?"

It is important to emphasise this callousness in Hamlet;

---

[1] That Hamlet fully shared his day's contempt for the acting profession is shown in III.2 when he asks Horatio whether his success in unmasking the King would not get him "a fellowship in a cry of players". The word *cry* could not be more contemptuous.

21

for unless it be adequately estimated his many deeds
remain incoherent and the very core of his character disintegrates. It is one of the two chief elements which explain
the scene of Polonius' death and the many references to
Polonius which Hamlet makes later. The other element is
the quickness and savagery of Hamlet's reactions when his
own skin (moral or physical) is threatened. The best
example in the whole play is perhaps this dramatic death of
Polonius. The scene cannot last more than fifteen to twenty
seconds. With the utmost skill Shakespeare starts the scare
in the woman. The Queen is frightened when Hamlet,
seizing her arm, says:

Come, come and sit you down, you shall not budge,

and she cries:

What wilt thou do? Thou wilt not murder me?
Help, help, ho!

Her "jumpy" state affects him; so that, when Polonius,
behind the arras, repeats the cry of help, he thinks the King
is behind, fears an instant danger, takes action first and kills
the old man. This is the irrational reaction less of actual fear
than of too close an approach to the sacred self.

And once the deed done, what sort of a funeral oration
does Polonius get?

Thou wretched, rash, intruding fool, farewell!
I took thee for thy better, take thy fortune,
Thou find'st to be too busy in some danger.

And that is all. But note that for Hamlet, the King, that
is, his own father's murderer, is the 'better' of Polonius,
the father of Ophelia: i.e. that Hamlet's scale of value is
not one of merit, virtue; but of power, *virtù*. We find again
the Renaissance Borgian philosophy, the philosophy of
success, expressed not as a thought consciously held, but
as a belief taken for granted. That Hamlet, the Borgian,
is the natural, spontaneous one. The Hamlet who preaches
to his mother must be left for a later page. Carried away
by his sermon, his eyes fall on Polonius' body, a mute witness who refutes his eloquent moralisations with a silent

"what about you?" And so Hamlet, answering Polonius,
says to his mother:

> For this same lord
> I do repent; but heaven hath pleased it so,
> To punish me with this, and this with me,
> That I must be their scourge and minister.
> I will bestow him, and will answer well
> The death I gave him;

This, however, is but a passing mood, born of his ser-
monising attitude to his mother. A moment later, when the
thought of Rosencrantz and Guildenstern has brought his
Borgian self back to the surface, he takes on again his
callous, cynical attitude towards his victim:

> This man shall set me packing
> I'll lug the guts into the neighbour room;
> Mother, good night indeed. This counsellor
> Is now most still, most secret, and most grave,
> Who was in life a foolish prating knave . . .
> Come, sir, to draw toward an end with you . . .
>
> (III.4.211-16).

And he leaves the room dragging 'the guts'.

It should be noted that this heartless exhibition of
callousness and cynicism has nothing to do with madness.
Hamlet has just agreed with his mother that she is not to
betray to the King:

> That I essentially am not in madness,
> But mad in craft.

The point is important in itself, because it shows that
Hamlet behaves in this inhuman fashion out of the very
exuberance of his Renaissance-Borgian indifference to any
other human being than himself. It is also important in
order to offset the argument that in his attitude when cross-
examined by the King on Polonius, he is just playing madness. Even if this were the case, it would argue a singular
freedom from feeling and respect; but, as a matter of fact,
the parting words to his mother are as callous and cynical
as his remarks to the King, so that the explanation is useless.

This scene with the King is magnificent as drama, and Hamlet's words are as felicitous as they are unforgettable. But the whole picture is based on Hamlet's self-centred freedom from any feeling for others; and to the end, he remains master of his wits and of his wit. "A' will stay till you come!" he shouts at Rosencrantz and Guildenstern as they leave to fetch the body.

§ 6. Laertes.

"That is Laertes, a very noble youth—mark." Such are the words in which Hamlet describes Laertes to Horatio in the Churchyard scene. With those words, Shakespeare provides us with a key to the relations between the two young men. Within a few minutes, Hamlet having come forward to provoke him (we shall soon hear him explain why), Laertes is at his throat. These are the cases when Hamlet reacts swiftly and savagely. "The devil take thy soul", Laertes has said, and Hamlet answers with singular moderation:

Thou pray'st not well.
I prithee take thy fingers from my throat,
For though I am not splenetive and rash
Yet have I in me something dangerous,
Which let thy wiseness fear; hold off thy hand.

The reason for this relative moderation though reacting to a direct attack, is that in this scene provocation starts on his side. As he puts it later to Horatio (V.2):

But I am very sorry, good Horatio,
That to Laertes I forgot myself;
For by the image of my cause I see
The portraiture of his; I'll court his favours:
But sure the bravery of his grief did put me
Into a towering passion.

This speech is full of information. It explains the true cause of the unseemly brawl at the grave; a mere rivalry over passion and even over a show of passion. Hamlet was not to be outdone by Laertes at anything, not excluding the expression of his love for Ophelia. Here, the feature now

24

twice observed, Hamlet's quick reaction against any aggression, is seen in another form: he gets into "a towering passion" at being challenged in feelings by Laertes. Note the word 'towering', which marvellously renders his sub-conscious motive: to out-do or excel Laertes and 'forty thousand' like him.

The next point to be gathered from this short speech is that Hamlet harbours some sympathy towards Laertes because he realises the parallel between their two 'causes', i.e. both are sons of murdered fathers. There is in Hamlet a secret envy of these young men, Fortinbras, Laertes, who go to action straightforwardly, without "thinking too precisely on th'event." (IV.4). While he . . . And there is also the sense that Laertes, like he himself, is one of the elect, not one of "the baser nature." This can be felt twice: in the way the words *very noble* come at once to his mind, when Hamlet speaks of Laertes for the first time: "That is Laertes, a very noble youth—mark"; and in the fact that the above quoted speech expressing regret, is obviously in opposition and contrast to all he has been saying about Rosencrantz and Guildenstern. Though there has gone between the two an eight-line speech on the King, it is possible to see Hamlet's trend from "They are not in my conscience (...) 'Tis dangerous when the baser nature comes between (...) mighty opposites" and "But I am very sorry, good Horatio that to Laertes I forgot myself." Hamlet remains faithful to his aristocratic, Borgian view of life.

Of course, we must not attribute to these values a modern sense, nor imagine that when Hamlet calls Laertes "a very noble youth" he takes a snobbish attitude. We have seen him appraise the difference between Polonius and the King, Polonius' "better"; while in the case of Laertes, who in point of 'nobility' is Polonius' son and no more, Hamlet gives the impression of treating him as an equal. Logically there is a contradiction between the two cases. But in Hamlet's mind there is none, for he is thinking in an intuitive way which combines both standards: family blood and personal *virtù*.

When Laertes leaps to his throat he feels, then, that he, Hamlet, by coming forward, has provoked Laertes; and he feels Laertes is "a very noble youth." The attack on his skin is not sudden enough, it does not come clean enough from the outside for him to retort with his usual savage swiftness.

Moreover, he does carry out the policy he had announced to Horatio: he does "court his favours." This has become indispensable for him. He has come back to Elsinore, whence he had been cast by the King with so much relief; and in this court, where he has no friend left but the power-less Horatio—rather a dialogue-prop than a character—he has foolishly alienated the young knight whose forceful personality is his only possible rival on the public stage. Policy then is the true motive power of his seemingly handsome apology to Laertes before the fencing in V.2; and when his mother sends him a message "to use some gentle entertainment to Laertes before you fall to play" he readily acquiesces since he had already announced to Horatio that he intended to "court his favours". So court he does with no uncertain tongue.

> Give me your pardon, sir. I have done you wrong,
> But pardon't, as you are a gentleman.
> This presence knows, and you must needs have heard,
> How I am punished with a sore distraction.
> What I have done
> That might your nature, honour and exception
> Roughly awake, I here proclaim was madness.
> Was't Hamlet wronged Laertes? never Hamlet.
> If Hamlet from himself be ta'en away,
> And when he's not himself does wrong Laertes,
> Then Hamlet does it not, Hamlet denies it.
> Who does it then? his madness. If't be so,
> Hamlet is of the faction that is wronged,
> His madness is poor Hamlet's enemy.
> Sir, in this audience,

Let my disclaiming from a purposed evil
Free me so far in your most generous thoughts,
That I have shot my arrow o'er the house,
And hurt my brother.

Now this is a most remarkable statement for Hamlet to make; so remarkable that it has puzzled Dr. Johnson and troubled Bradley. "I wish Hamlet had made some other defence; it is unsuitable to the character of a brave or a good man to shelter himself in falsehood," comments Dr. Johnson. But who said that Hamlet was 'a brave or a good man'? Not Shakespeare. What Shakespeare says is that Hamlet excuses himself—of what, we shall discuss anon—by putting it all to the debit of his madness.

The view has been put forward that Hamlet cannot be lying or simulating at this moment of the play, for at this moment above all others the poet is anxious to secure our admiration and sympathy for him.[1] But again Shakespeare does not take sides between Hamlet and Laertes. We are also told that when Hamlet "stands away from the grave quivering (...) the ranting insincerity of Laertes has become commonplace and contemptible beside the agony of this great and tortured spirit."[2] No such conclusion can be countenanced by an impartial reader or spectator. Laertes loved Ophelia even though Shakespeare does not manage to express this love in the best taste; Hamlet is raving about himself, thinking and feeling of himself, relieving his sense of guilt about Ophelia. Shakespeare remains faithful to his pattern—nothing but Hamlet can arouse Hamlet.

And, of course, once this is understood, the speech of excuse stands in a clearer light. True, it brings out the contrast between Hamlet's attitude and that of Laertes just before a fight in which Laertes means foul play. But Hamlet does not come to the meeting in a mood

Most generous and free from all contriving.

He comes to court Laertes' favours. He has told us so

[1] D.W., p. 217.
[2] D.W., p. 271.

himself. He must win back Laertes. Hence this speech. To describe it as "a noble and touching plea for forgiveness and for affection" is, with all respect, a monument of pro-Hamlet bias. The speech is an admirable example of egotism. Hamlet has provoked an unseemly brawl at the churchyard when Laertes' sister was being buried; he has wronged this sister and driven her to madness and death; and he has killed Laertes' father; and then he coolly comes with hands stretched to Laertes and says: 'Pardon me. I have done you wrong. You know I am subject to a sore distraction. Let us be brothers.' Could self-centredness go further? Why, shedding tears of repentance on his knees before Laertes, Hamlet would not have humbled himself enough to merit forgiveness for the burden of his offences; and because he is Hamlet and all is allowed him, an excuse of 'sore distraction' is to wipe out his crime and his insolence—and this is "generous" and "noble"!

Noble and generous he certainly thought he was, and that was part of his tragedy. For he was unable to see why Laertes should not accept his "brotherly" offer of peace since he—like the Frenchman in the story—felt no resentment against those he had wronged. For him, the death of Polonius, the wrongs done to Ophelia and his insulting of Laertes at his sister's grave were just outward events; they did not concern him deeply. He therefore dismissed them lightly; and as a true egotist, having dismissed them, he saw no reason why Laertes should not do as much. Such is the true psychological background of this speech.

There is, of course, an intensely dramatic contrast between the two men who exchange a few words before crossing foils; but not that of a white, spontaneous and generous Hamlet versus a black "insincere" and "scheming false-faced opponent". Shakespeare was too subtle for sheer black versus white. When Hamlet and Laertes meet, the drama lies in that Hamlet is so blinded by his egotism that he does not realise Laertes' state of mind and thinks he can square him by a show of reconciliation and affection, partly genuine but mostly acted; while the audience knows that Laertes cannot be so fobbed off.

Nor is it possible to follow those who conclude that "when Hamlet tells us that he is subject to 'a sore distraction' and killed Polonius in madness we are expected to believe him."[1] This cannot have been Shakespeare's intention, for at least two reasons: the first is that Hamlet does not offer madness to Laertes as the reason for Polonius' death only, but for:

> What I have done
> That might your nature, honour and exception
> Roughly awake;

to wit: "nature", for Polonius and Ophelia; "honour" for Ophelia; "exception" for the brawl; and Hamlet could not sincerely allege madness for *all* these, though there was enough excitability in him to enable him to call it madness when necessary by a process of exaggeration rather than by sheer lying; and the second reason is that Hamlet has already told his mother that he is only mad in craft.

Note the word: craft. It is Hamlet who uses it to describe his own behaviour. And set it beside his own words to Horatio, "I'll court his favours" to describe what his policy towards Laertes is going to be. There *is* policy; there *is* craft. Hamlet seizes hold of "madness" as he would of any other pretext to get round Laertes. He is "courting" his favours, and we all know what insincerity, craft, intrigue, these two words 'court' and 'favour' called forth in the minds of all Elizabethans. This much can be said without further proof. But there is further proof that Hamlet is dissembling to Laertes. Here it is.

Hamlet to *Laertes:*

> I'll be your foil, Laertes. In mine ignorance
> Your skill shall like a star i'th'darkest night
> Stick fiery off indeed.

---

[1] It is even doubtful whether Dr. Dover Wilson, the leader of this way of thinking, follows his own opinion; for p. 223 he writes: "The killing of Polonius, which Hamlet here attributes to his madness, is not felt to be an insane action while we witness it, not pathologically insane, though we are quite ready to accept Hamlet's word for its insanity an hour later." And, still uneasy, he adds in a foot note. "In the theatre, that is; in the study the artifice shows a little too nakedly."

Hamlet in conversation with Horatio a few minutes earlier:

Horatio: You will lose this wager, my Lord.

Hamlet: I do not think so. Since he went into France, I have been in continual practice. I shall win at the odds.

These two utterances a few minutes from each other prove beyond dispute that Hamlet is determined to win Laertes' favour without stopping at the borders of truth. He flatters him extravagantly, comparing his adversary's skill to a star in the night of his own ignorance; and in so doing reveals to the attentive spectator or reader his usual free and egotistic stand above facts and persons. For under his heavy flattery of Laertes there lies, of course, an utter indifference and even contempt for the man he is thus stuffing with unmeant words. This feature again is true to type, as shown by his identical attitude towards Rosencrantz and Guildenstern, Polonius, Osric whom he delightfully and deliciously plays with but treats with no human consideration whatever, and indeed every man with whom he comes in touch.

The end of his relations with Laertes proves nothing. Laertes wounds him slightly; this, of course, brings out a savage and swift reaction in Hamlet since it reveals foul play, which leads to the exchange of weapons and to Laertes' death. Every healthy man would have reacted as Hamlet; but the fact remains that even here, he remains true to type and is aroused to violence as soon as his skin is touched.

CHAPTER II

HAMLET AND OPHELIA:

ENIGMAS AND THEIR KEY

§ 1. *The Sentimental Falsification.*

We have so far brought out into sharp relief that backbone of Hamlet's character without which his words and deeds are incoherent. It had remained unrecognised owing to the widespread prejudice in favour of Hamlet which has too often warped and obscured his character and the whole play; for it so happens that this utterly self-centred attitude, often undistinguishable from mere selfishness, was a far less disreputable feature in Shakespeare's aesthetical days than it is in our ethical times. But, of course, essential as it is, this egotism of Hamlet is but his psychological backbone; and to make up the whole there remain many other features, over which there is hardly a difference of opinion nowadays. They are the powers and graces of the most fascinating character of the European stage.

This fascination which Hamlet exerts on all has power-fully contributed to the misunderstanding which prevails over his relations with Ophelia. The critic starts with the prepossession that these relations must satisfy the standards of a cultivated, refined, honest, 'decent' gentleman of his contemporary Britain; and when he comes across facts and words which do not tally in the least with his prepossession, he just stalls. It is crucial to begin by emphasising this fact: orthodox criticism of Hamlet has failed to provide a coherent explanation of the Hamlet-Ophelia problem. Critics are surprised, puzzled, pained, offended; they offer us feelings galore: ideas, few that can stand the facts. When, therefore, we attempt to build up an interpretation of this problem, consistent not only in itself, but also with Shakespeare's text, and with all we already know of Hamlet's character, we are not "looking for noon at fourteen" as the French might say, or seeking to go one better than those who have already solved the problem to everybody's satisfaction: we are endeavouring to fill up a void. This, one of the most haunting questions in the most haunting European tragedy, is still unsolved.

Nor is Hamlet's own singular charm the only magnet which has deflected the light of criticism from its true course. The chief cause of the trouble may well be the height of poetical power and pathos to which Shakespeare raises the play in the scene of Ophelia's madness; the songs, the flowers, "the pity of it", work our emotions to such a pitch and tension that Ophelia is thereby transfigured and her whole life is retrospectively coloured by this hectic sunset of her mind. By a curious effect of this alchemy, not only Ophelia but Hamlet as well becomes transfigured and sentimentalised. And so, Ophelia has been established as the paragon of innocence, love and undeserved tragedy, not very clever perhaps, but so sweet! As for Hamlet, it soon became a habit to convey to the audience, by some tender gesture when Ophelia was not looking, that though he might speak harsh and insulting words to her, he still at heart loved her. The masterpiece of this extravagant distortion of Shakespeare's intentions was performed by Edmund Kean. Hackett describes him, at the end of the 'nunnery' scene, coming back to "smother Ophelia's hand with passionate kisses".[1] "He brought to Hamlet"—writes Mr. Harold Child—"certain things which others were glad to take over from him, notably an emphasis (...) on Hamlet's abiding passion for Ophelia, which led him to treat her without 'the conventional coarseness and almost brutal ferocity', and to come back to her at the end of the 'nunnery' scene and kiss her hand."[2]

This is a valuable revelation, rendered more valuable

[1] J. H. Hackett quoted by Furness, vol. II, p. 251.

[2] D.W.H., lxxxviii.

still by a further point of history Mr. Harold Child supplies in a parenthesis: "Writing in 1812, Lamb had protested against that convention, thus proving its prevalence." This shows that what Lamb and Mr. Harold Child call a "convention", and was really a stage-tradition, whereby Hamlet treated Ophelia with a coarseness and a brutality in complete harmony with the text, persisted down to Kean's days; and that it was the romantic era, with its tendency to escape from the facts, that brought forth the critic—Lamb —and the actor—Kean—responsible for the falsification of this deeply human theme. No doubt the tendency was there before Lamb and Kean came to bestow upon it a kind of official sanction. Garrick, we are told, struck some critics as boisterous and harsh[1] towards Ophelia. But the new stage tradition with its sentimental and false belief in "Hamlet's abiding passion for Ophelia" dates from the romantic measles of the XIXth century.

§ 2. *Barbarous and Supersubtle.*

Let us go back to the XVIth century. "It is a mistake, of which some modern critics are guilty, to try to fit Shakespeare's creatures and his conceptions of human nature into the procrustean bed of Elizabethan psychology; his visions altogether transcended such limitations. But it is equally unfortunate to leave contemporary notions of the kind out of our reckoning in estimating his dramatic situations. Elizabethan psychology helps us little to solve the mystery of Hamlet; but some knowledge of it is essential to the full understanding of what the other characters in the play think about him and his behaviour."[2] These words clearly define the position. One might perhaps have wished for greater emphasis on the value of Elizabethan psychology to understand Hamlet's "mystery" as well; for transcend as Shakespeare may his time and country, in his thoughts and conceptions, he was steeped in them and could not fail

[1] D.W.H., lxxx.
[2] D.W., p. 117.

33

to take his cues, his background, his axioms and assumptions from the environment in which he lived.

What was this environment like? "The ultimate fact"— writes J. M. Robertson—"is that Shakespeare *could not* make a psychologically or otherwise consistent play out of a plot which retained a strictly barbaric action while the hero was transformed into a supersubtle Elizabethan."[1] This at any rate, is clear, and we know where we stand. We stand among those who say outright that Robertson is mistaken; that *Hamlet* is a perfectly consistent play; and that an era can be at the same time barbarous and supersubtle. Cesare Borgia was both, magnificently. So were Queen Elizabeth herself, and most of her contemporaries. "What kind of mental fabric could that have been which had for its warp the habits of filth and savagery of sixteen-century London and for its woof an impassioned familiarity with the splendour of *Tamburlaine* and the exquisiteness of *Venus and Adonis?* Who can reconstruct those iron-nerved beings who passed with rapture from some divine madrigal sung to a lute by a bewitching boy in a tavern to the spectacle of mauled dogs tearing a bear to pieces? (...). And the curious society which loved such fantasies and delicacies—how readily would it turn and rend a random victim with hideous cruelty! A change of fortune—a spy's word—and those same ears might be sliced off, to the laughter of the crowd, in the pillory; or, if ambition or religion made a darker embroilment, a more ghastly mutilation might diversify a traitor's end."[2]

This picture from the pen of a connoisseur of Elizabethan times is enough to prove that nothing is too barbarous to happen in *Hamlet*. The same author may enable us to understand the environment in which Hamlet and Ophelia were born. Queen Elizabeth had been doomed to a sad, tense and hectic amorous life by both nature and nurture. "She was not yet fifteen, and was living in the house of her

[1] The Problem of Hamlet, p. 74, quoted by D.W., p. 14.

[2] E.E.S., pp. 9–20.

stepmother, Katherine Parr, who had married the Lord
Admiral Seymour, brother of Somerset, the Protector. The
Admiral was handsome, fascinating and reckless; he amused
himself with the princess. Bounding into her room in the
early morning, he would fall upon her, while she was in her
bed or just out of it, with peals of laughter, would seize her
in his arms and tickle her, and slap her buttocks, and crack
a ribald joke."[1] This led to rumours that she was with child
by him, which though unfounded, cost Seymour his head.
His brother the Protector, who ordered his execution, was
by no means upholding "morals" thereby; he was getting
rid of a rival ready to climb to power by way of princely
bedrooms.

When on the throne, Elizabeth succeeded in procrastinating about her marriage till it ceased to be politically
necessary in order to guarantee a direct succession. Her
aversion to matrimony is generally believed to have been
due to some bodily maladjustment or defect which made
actual procreative intercourse repellent while, however,
whetting and exasperating appetite. This led to turning the
court into an inverted farmyard, where the hen-Queen
played cock to a host of cock-courtiers playing hens to her.
The outcome of it all is best described by the same connoisseur: "Though, at the centre of her being, desire had
turned to repulsion, it had not vanished altogether; on the
contrary, the compensating forces of nature had redoubled
its vigour elsewhere. Though the precious citadel itself was
never to be violated, there were surrounding territories,
there were outworks and bastions over which exciting
battles might be fought, and which might even, at moments,
be allowed to fall into the bold hands of an assailant.
Inevitably, strange rumours flew. The princely suitors multi-
plied their assiduities; and the Virgin Queen alternately
frowned and smiled over her secret."[2]

That was the model, that "the glass of fashion and the

[1] E.E.S., *loc. cit.*

[2] E.E.S., p. 25.

mould of form" which the whole society in which *Hamlet* was conceived, followed and imitated. It is unhistorical to turn away from it, and to pretend that the scenes in which Hamlet and Ophelia speak the language of that society, before an audience of that society, have nothing to do with, do not refer to such a mode of living. Hamlet and Ophelia were two contemporaries of Raleigh, Essex, Blount and the girls who played with them—if and when the Queen allowed her swains to wander away from the royal "outworks and bastions". The whole audience knew what the Court was like, and lived in very much the same way. The situations on the stage, the words, the hints, the gestures were all related to similar situations, words, hints and gestures, familiar to the Court and by no means caviare to the general.

§ 3. *Did Hamlet love Ophelia?*

So far the background and the perspective. Next comes getting rid of irrelevant notions. There are two such notions which encumber the fair ground: one is Hamlet's love and the other is Ophelia's candour.

"That Hamlet was at one time genuinely in love with Ophelia"—writes an eminent authority—"no serious critic has, I think, ever questioned."[1] Then I am no serious critic, for I hold that Hamlet never was meant by Shakespeare to have been in love with Ophelia. Indeed the idea that Hamlet could be in love at all with anybody but himself is incompatible with Hamlet's character. This is an assertion we already are entitled to make, since we have proved that Hamlet is a self-centred character and since we know that Shakespeare knew what he was about. But (according to the rules of this game known as literary criticism) it is an assertion which had better be proved on its own ground by means of quotations from the play. Now, whatever the circumstances, whatever the excuses, is it possible that a man who had loved a woman should treat her as Hamlet treats Ophelia repeatedly? Are the 'nunnery' scene and the conversation at

[1] D.W., p. 108

the play reconcilable even with a love that is past? "Hamlet"
—writes the same authority—"treats Ophelia like a prostitute"; and while in this, the eminent critic may go too far,
his award is surely proof enough that Hamlet had never
loved Ophelia! For, no matter her crimes, and we have seen
her commit none so far to justify Hamlet's behaviour, a
man of Hamlet's stamp would demean himself by "treating
like a prostitute" a woman he had once loved.

But that is not all. For surely a true love, even if extinct,
would leave behind enough embers of respect towards the
once beloved and towards her family. Now, Polonius might
be garrulous and meddlesome, but he was the father of
Ophelia. He might conspire to test Hamlet by eavesdropping; but that was not such a crime as to justify the
gibes, the mockery, the actual insults to an old man who
was the father of the once beloved. And the callous words
he addresses the body after slaying him behind the arras—
not a thought for Ophelia then!—and that gruesome line:
    I'll lug the guts into the neighbour room
and that stark stage direction "*he drags the body from the
room*", are any of these things compatible even with extinct
love?[1]

Shakespeare did everything he could to convey to his
audience the fact that Hamlet had never loved Ophelia.
True he makes Ophelia speak of the "words of so sweet
breath composed"; note she speaks of *words;* true he says:
I did love you once, but this whole dialogue to which we must
return, ends with a remarkable exchange of hard truths:
"*I loved you not*," says Hamlet, and Ophelia retorts: "*I was
the more deceived.*" The only other pronouncement on the
subject we hear from Hamlet's own lips in his frantic:
    I loved Ophelia, forty thousand brothers

---

[1] The Globe stage direction: "Exeunt severally: Hamlet dragging in Polonius" is not explicit in Q_2
but is implied, since Hamlet has announced that he "will lug the guts into the neighbour room",
and, of course, Polonius must be removed from the then curtainless stage. F_1 says: "Exit Hamlet
tugging in Polonius". The Queen, however, removes all doubts in IV.1 for to the King's "Where is
he gone?" she answers
    To draw apart the body he hath kill'd
and the King says later to Rosencrantz and Guildenstern:
    Hamlet in madness hath Polonius slain,
    And from his mother's closet hath he dragg'd him.

Could not with all their quality of love
Make up my sum—

words which were certainly not meant to convey to anyone
in his senses that Hamlet loved Ophelia; but merely that
he was ready to outdo Laertes in anything, from loving
Ophelia to drinking vinegar or ranting as well as any man.
Whether the struggle between the two takes place in the
grave or—as some prefer—out of it, the tradition which
makes Hamlet and Laertes fight over the body of Ophelia
is sound, for it materialises and symbolises in a striking
manner the cockfight between the two young bloods in utter
oblivion and disregard of the occasion—not the cause—of
it: the dead young woman.

It might be argued—if with but little force—that all this
happens when Hamlet has already lost his love for Ophelia.
But lest we were thus led astray, Shakespeare took care to
provide us with a first-hand document of the period before,
on any hypothesis, his love had "ceased". Hamlet's love
letter which Polonius reads to the King and Queen in II.2
raises one of the many problems in Shakespeare. Polonius
brings it in triumph to the King after the scene in which
Ophelia "affrighted" reports Hamlet's sudden visit to her.
When was this letter written? Recently? But how could
Hamlet play with such "numbers" when he was so sorely
tried by the revelations of the Ghost? And how could
Ophelia possess it since in the previous scene she tells her
father "I did repel his letters"?[1] Was then the letter old,
previous to the King's murder? But then how is it Polonius
makes news of it? Shakespeare is precise in essence, vague
in detail. The solution is this: the letter is old. Polonius lies
when he says it was given him by his daughter "in her duty
and obedience". We know he lies because the vain old man
goes on to say:

This in obedience hath my daughter shown me,
And more above hath his solicitings,

---

[1] This, however, by itself, would not be a strong enough argument, for, as shown under § 4 below, Ophelia is not sincere in her promises to her father.

> As they fell out by time, by means and place,
>   All given to mine ear

which we know is not true, since we have heard father and
daughter talk the matter *over* but—so far as Ophelia is
concerned—by no means *out*. Furthermore, Polonius goes
on to say:

> When I had seen this hot love on the wing
> As I perceived it (I must tell you that)
> Before my daughter told me . . .

and we know because we heard the old man say so himself,
that his friends had to warn him of what was going on before
he bethought himself of asking his daughter "What is between you?" Polonius must have pried into Ophelia's papers,
and, having found the letter, taken it to parade before the
King with it. This enables him to prove his shrewdness in
guessing that Hamlet was mad for love of Ophelia without
revealing Hamlet's visit to Ophelia, which would prove it
better still, but would leave him in the position of a father
whose daughter, despite his boasts, was not well guarded.

All this goes to show that this letter comes from the
period before the play, when, if ever Hamlet was in love
with Ophelia, no cloud had come to disturb his feelings.
Now, is this a love letter at all? There are eminent authorities—Dowden one of them—who say it is. No girl of
average feminine acumen would take such stuff for the style
of love. "To the celestial, and my soul's idol, the most
beautified Ophelia" might do for Osric; but from Hamlet's
pen it can only mean *fun*. He is having fun out of her as he
does out of everybody; playing *on* her as if she were an
instrument. The mood is the same as that of his talk to,
or rather, through, Osric. "Most beautified Ophelia" does
mean "most made-up Ophelia"; not merely because it tallies
with "I have heard of your paintings" at III.1, but (which
is even more to the point) because Hamlet was not a man
who could write *beautified* when he meant *beautiful;* so that
the argument that "Polonius' condemnation of 'beautified'
is sufficient to show that it is an innocent word" should be

inverted: it shows that Hamlet did not mean it in the sense
in which Polonius rightly criticised it. Then come four lines
of doggerel which Hamlet must have known had nothing to
do with either genuine love or genuine poetry:

> Doubt thou the stars are fire
> Doubt that the sun doth move,
> Doubt truth to be a liar
> But never doubt I love.

and then the "Oh bother" perfunctory paragraph: "O dear
Ophelia, I am ill at these numbers, I have not art to reckon
my groans, but that I love thee best, O most best, believe it.
Adieu. Thine evermore, most dear lady, whilst this machine
is to him, Hamlet."

If that is the way Shakespeare made Hamlet express his
love for Ophelia, he who has endowed the English language
with one of the richest anthologies of love the world pos-
sesses, from the adolescent love of Romeo to the autumnal
and hectic love of Anthony, we are right in concluding that
Hamlet was at no time in love with Ophelia.

§ 4. Did Ophelia Love Hamlet and Was She Candid?

One thing is certain: Ophelia was not candid towards
Hamlet. She allowed herself to be used as a decoy to enable
her father and the King to overhear the conversation with
the man we are asked—though not by Shakespeare—to
believe that she was in love with. This is a pretty broad hint
on the part of the author. It means: "You people down there
in the pit, keep an eye on this girl. She looks ever so sweet.
But you need not believe anything she says."

Had critics paid more heed to this tacit warning, they
would have avoided two pitfalls: that of believing she loved
Hamlet and that of reading into her a virginal innocence
and a candour which Shakespeare never dreamt she should
possess.

That she was not in love with him is proved by her very

acquiescence in her father's designs. Any young woman with a genuine love for a man would have resisted the part assigned to her in that comedy, and instinctively sided with her lover against the two "lawful espials". She makes no opposition whatever and she enters fully into the plot. Weakness? Were it so, Shakespeare would have shown somewhere at some time, the smarting of her heart at her betrayal. Moreover, Ophelia was not weak. She knew how to keep her counsel.

We are advised by an authority on Hamlet to bear in mind that, in order not to misunderstand the 'nunnery' scene we must remember that it is not Hamlet who has repelled Ophelia but Ophelia Hamlet.[1] What evidence is there for such a conclusion? Let us listen to the play: We first hear of Hamlet's interest in Ophelia when Laertes gives her advice about it, prolix enough to augur for the young man as garrulous an old age as his father's. What is her reaction? Does she raise the slightest objection to all the indirect accusations against Hamlet implicit in her brother's sermon? None. All she offers is a formal and outward acquiescence. Not a shadow of a suggestion that she loves him. And, most revealing of all, these lines:

> But good my brother
> Do not, as some ungracious pastors do,
> Show me the steep and thorny way to heaven,
> Whiles like a puffed and reckless libertine
> Himself the primrose path of dalliance treads
> And recks not his own rede.

Could Shakespeare give us a broader hint on what was in Ophelia's mind and on the way she conceived her own relations with Hamlet?

Then, Laertes gone, Polonius takes on the subject again, in a scene in which, again, Ophelia gives not a shadow of a sign, direct or indirect, that she is in love with Hamlet. As for his love for her, she reports:

> He hath, my lord, of late, made many tenders

[1] D.W., p. 127.

41

Of his affection to me.

Asked whether she believes in them, Ophelia answers:

I do not know, my Lord, what I should think,

which is probably true. Then she says: "He hath importuned me with love in honourable fashion"; "And hath given countenance to his speech with almost all the holy vows of heaven." Finally, when ordered no longer "to give words or talk with the Lord Hamlet", she promptly bows: "I shall obey, my lord."

The next thing that happens is Hamlet's dramatic, silent visit to her which she comes, still 'affrighted', to report to her father (II.1). "Mad for thy love?"—he asks; and she, who knows better, answers ambiguously: "My Lord, I do not know but truly I do fear it." Then Polonius asks an extraordinary question:

What, have you given him any hard words of late?

This shows how little faith the old man laid in his daughter's obedience. But she dutifully answers:

No, my good Lord, but as you did command,
I did repel his letters, and denied
His access to me.

That is what she says to her father. But can it be true? Evidently not. For were it true, she would not return the trinkets alleging that:

Rich gifts wax poor when givers prove unkind!

This little scene proves that Ophelia had paid no notice either to her brother's or to her father's sermons; that she promised Laertes with her lips what she was determined not to carry out; and that she bowed at once with a 'I shall obey' to her father's orders not to receive Hamlet, because she had not the slightest intention of obeying them. If this interpretation is not accepted, the trinkets scene has no sense.

Ophelia is in fact a flirt; a fast girl such as at Elizabeth's court was the rule rather than the exception; a girl whose model was Ann Boleyn, the young beauty who ascended the throne by way of the King's bedroom. This much can be

concluded from all that precedes. An examination of the play
scene will confirm it. The very first words and action of
Hamlet with regard to Ophelia in this scene confirm our
view of their relationship. "Come hither, my dear Hamlet,
sit by me," says the Queen; and he, sitting at Ophelia's
feet, retorts: "No, good mother, here is metal more attractive." This disposes of all explanations which would account
for Hamlet's brutality towards Ophelia by dividing their
relationship into two phases: a love-phase and a no-love
or even hate-phase. No. After their 'nunnery' scene and a
few seconds before that obscene dialogue during the play
scene, Ophelia is attractive metal to Hamlet. Their relationship was ever the same: one which enabled Hamlet to
write a mock-and-bother letter during the "love" period,
and to seek her company during the "no-love" period; in
fact, one of neither love nor no-love, hereafter to be analysed.

Then comes the obscene dialogue; for it is a dialogue.
Now if Ophelia was the innocent, candid maid she is sup-
posed to be, this dialogue could not have gone beyond the
"I think nothing, my Lord"; the only decent answer
Ophelia gives Hamlet in the scene. But what sort of maiden's
innocence is it which, to:

> That's a fair thought to lie between maid's legs,

asks:

> What is, my Lord?

These four words should have been enough to reveal
Ophelia's true character to all but hopeless romantics and
sentimentalists. And to Hamlet's "Nothing", Ophelia comments: "You are merry, my Lord." Let critics think that
he is "disgusting", "insulting" and "gross";[1] but Ophelia
just thinks he is "merry". And this difference in words
measures the difference in values between the XIXth
century critic and the XVIth century author: Hamlet does
not treat Ophelia like a prostitute; he treats her as a young
Elizabethan courtier would a young Elizabethan flirt with
no particular inhibition about anything.

[1] Bradley, p. 103.

A girl of the stamp orthodox critics still see in Ophelia would either have left the room, or moved away from Hamlet or never addressed a word to him after his obscene opening gambit. Ophelia talks and even engages him in conversation when he is silent, as if wanting more "insults". She asks "What means this, my Lord?" and "Will a'tell us what this show meant?" To which Hamlet answers, not in the least "savagely", but in the same jesting-indecent-sardonic mood: "Ay, or any show that you'll show him; be not you ashamed to show, he'll not shame to tell you what it means."

To this, she comments: "You are naught, you are naught, I'll mark the play"—which in the circumstances is downright encouragement. But he has of course other things to attend to; so she has to wait till a later phase, when Hamlet having explained

This is one Lucianus, nephew to the King,
the much insulted but never enough insulted young lady, puts in: "You are as good as a chorus, my Lord". This brings him out in his best form: "I could interpret between you and your love, if I could see the puppets dallying".

Could any one in his senses believe that this man had ever been in love with the woman to whom he spoke thus? And how revealing her answer: "You are keen, my Lord, you are keen". This answer shatters the accepted view that she is undeservedly repelled. He treats her "love" as a puppet show and she—well, does she not acknowledge that he is not altogether mistaken? Then, Hamlet goes on worse: "It would cost you a groaning to take off my edge" —a remark she ought not to understand, were she "sweet, innocent Ophelia"; but which simply delights her, for she answers: "Still better and worse". That is: "You are naught, but I like it."

§ 5. *Hamlet's Attitude Unexplained.*

The enigmas in Hamlet's behaviour towards Ophelia proved a stumbling block for Bradley. "I am unable to arrive at a conviction as to the meaning of some of his words and deeds, and I question whether from the mere text of the play a sure interpretation of them can be drawn".[1] A remarkable confession of critical bankruptcy from so rich an intellect; the explanation of which can be found within a few lines. "On two points no reasonable doubt can, I think, be felt. Hamlet was at one time sincerely and ardently in love with Ophelia." And mark Bradley's *proof:* "For she herself says that he had importuned her with love in honourable fashion, and had given countenance to his speech with almost all the holy vows of heaven". Of course, a bank that would pay cash of faith for such paper money could not but fail. On such premises, Bradley examines the relations between Hamlet and Ophelia and can come to no adequate conclusion.

A not inconsiderable step forward has been made by Dr. Dover Wilson. According to him, the plot to spy on Hamlet while he talks to Ophelia, must have been overheard by the intended victim as Polonius expounds it in II.2. He rightly thinks that the words of Polonius

> You know, sometimes he walks for hours together
> Here in the lobby

are a signal to the audience to look where he comes reading, entering the inner stage by the door at the back while Polonius speaks on. This is an invaluable discovery which makes many things clearer, though perhaps not as many as its discoverer thinks. Admirably argued though it is, it may still be strengthened with one observation which goes to confirm it. The words of the Queen: "But look where sadly the poor wretch comes reading" would be useless unless they were intended to draw the attention of the two conspirators to the fact that he is coming—a fact discovered, if too late, precisely by the Queen. On the principle that Shakespeare always writes to some purpose, and wastes no breath in useless gossip, this line he gives the Queen, and this choice of the Queen for saying it, are tantamount to a proof that Dr. Dover Wilson is right.

[1] Bradley, p. 153 ss.

On this important elucidation, Dr. Dover Wilson builds up an explanation of Hamlet's attitude to Ophelia which may be summed up as follows:

1. Hamlet goes to see Ophelia in the distress of his soul, over the revelation of the Ghost. All he seeks is help from the woman he loves. Not yet suspicious of her, he is nevertheless already receptive to suspicion.

2. Hamlet overhears Polonius explain his plot about "lawful espials". This enrages Hamlet to the point of uttering his "fishmonger" string of obscenities, which, we are told, do not, "except indirectly, reflect upon Ophelia herself".

3. When in the decoy scene, Hamlet, while soliloquising on 'to be or not to be' suddenly sees Ophelia, "the sight reminds him of nothing except 'the pangs of disprised love' (. . .) she had refused to see him and had returned his letters; she could not speak a word of comfort when in deep trouble he found his way into her room with mute pitiable appeal. After that he had done with her". He sounds bored. Then Ophelia overplays her part and produces the trinkets. This reminds him of the plot. Ophelia *is* a decoy. This "play-acting has completed her downfall in his eyes". She "gets what she deserves", i.e. being treated as a whore and bid to go to a brothel.

4. In the play scene "his language to Ophelia, outrageous as it is, is in keeping with the part of a love-distraught swain."[1]

Let us now examine these four points:

1. On the scene in Ophelia's closet, Dr. Dover Wilson himself quotes an admirable statement of Dr. Bradley:

"When Hamlet made his way into Ophelia's room, why did he go in the garb, the conventionally recognised garb, of the distracted *lover?* If it was necessary to convince Ophelia of his insanity, how was it necessary to convince her that disappointment in *love* was the cause of his insanity? His *main* object in the visit appears to have been to convince

[1] D.W., pp. 111–112.

others, through her, that his insanity was not due to any mysterious unknown cause, but to this disappointment, and so to allay the suspicions of the King. But if his feeling for her had been simply that of love, however unhappy, and had not been in any degree that of suspicion or resentment, would he have adopted a plan which must involve her in so much suffering?"

This in unanswerable. Dr. Dover Wilson's explanation leaves the problem unsolved. He puts it all on to "disprised love". "Hamlet is of course deeply hurt by her refusal to see him and by the return of his letters; and this explains his silence and the passionate scrutiny of her face: he will not speak unless she first speaks to him". This is sheer romantic imagination, wholly out of touch with sixteenth-century life. We know Hamlet was not in love with Ophelia; we know she did not return his letters nor close her door to him; we know it because she implies as much in the 'nunnery' scene twice: when returning the trinkets and when greeting him with

> Good my Lord,
> How does your honour for this many a day;

which *proves* that her door had remained open but that he, his head full of other things of more import than Ophelia, had not come to see her for about two months. So number one will not do.

2. That Hamlet overhears the conversation in which Polonius plots to spy on him is a true contribution to this debate. But that this fact is enough to explain Hamlet's language in the "fishmonger's" episode cannot be accepted for a moment. Hamlet waxes obscene about Polonius and about Ophelia as well, and by no means indirectly, for there is no fishmonger without fish. This language, if based only on the idea that Ophelia was being used as a decoy, would be out of place even if, as we here maintain, Hamlet did not love, had never loved Ophelia; but if as late as in the play scene, Hamlet is still "love-distraught", it is simply impossible. So number two will not do.

47

3. Hamlet looks upon Ophelia as a stranger and sounds bored (this is excellent but hardly reconcilable with the rest of the explanation). Then the trinkets and Hamlet's explosion of gross insults. But how is it possible to argue that, *under any interpretation* so far given, Ophelia "gets what she deserves?" Does acting as decoy for her father and the King to find out what is wrong with him justify being treated as a whore and sent to a brothel? The answer is NO. So number three will not do.

4. Can the obscenities of Hamlet in the play scene be described as, though outrageous, in keeping with the part of a love-distraught swain? No. And was any love left in Hamlet for Ophelia in Dr. Dover Wilson's own interpretation? No. So number four will not do.

§ *6. The Sources.*

We are thus led to seek an explanation for this essential episode or aspect of the play, still a kind of *res nullius* of criticism. And at this stage we think it wise to seek our way by returning to the historical method. We know to what an extent Shakespeare's *Hamlet* borrows from Saxo Grammaticus and from Belleforest. A study of the Hamlet–Ophelia episode in these two sources might well prove fruitful. What do we find in Saxo Grammaticus? Amleth is a prince whose strange behaviour leads people to suspect that "his mind was quick enough", and that "he only played the simpleton in order to hide his understanding". These persons thought that "his wiliness would be most readily detected, if a fair woman were put in his way in some secluded place, who should provoke his mind to the temptations of love; all men's natural temper being too blindly amorous to be artfully dissembled". This was done. "The woman whom his uncle had despatched met him in a dark spot, as though she had crossed him by chance, and he took her and would have ravished her, had not his foster-brother, by a secret device, given him an inkling of the trap. (. . .) Alarmed, scenting a trap, and fain to possess his desire in

48

greater safety, he caught up the woman in his arms and dragged her off to a distant and impenetrable fen. Moreover, when they had lain together, he conjured her earnestly to disclose the matter to none, and the promise of silence was accorded as heartily as it was asked. For both of them had been under the same fostering in childhood; and this early rearing in common had brought Amleth and the girl into great intimacy. So, when he had returned home, they all jeeringly asked him whether he had given way to love, and he avowed that he had ravished the maid. (. . .) The maiden, too, when questioned on the matter, declared that he had done no such thing, and her denial was the more readily credited when it was found that the escort had not witnessed the deed."[1]

So far Saxo Grammaticus. As for Belleforest, he also begins by pointing out how, observing the Prince's pranks, "les hommes accors, et qui avoient le nez long, commencent à soupçonner ce qui estoit, et estimerent que sous ceste folie gisoit et estoit cachée une grande finesse. (. . .) A ceste cause donnerent conseil au Roy de tenter par tout moyen s'il se pourroit faire, que ce fard fust descouvert, et qu'on s'aperceust de la tromperie de l'adolescent. Or ne voyent ils ruse plus propre pour l'atraper, que s'ils luy mettoient quelque belle femme en lieu secret, laquelle taschast de le gaigner avec ses caresses les plus mignardes et attrayantes. (. . .) D'autant que le naturel de tout jeune homme, mesmement setant nourry à son aise est si transporté aux plaisirs de la chair (. . .) qu'il est presque impossible de couvrir telle affection, n'y d'en dissimuler les apprehensions par art. (. . .) Ainsi furent deputez quelques courtisans, pour mener le Prince en quelque lieu escarté, dans le boys, et lesquels luy presentassent ceste femme, l'incitans à se souiller en ses baysers et embrassemens, artifices assez frequent(s) de nostre temps, non pour essayer si les grands sont hors de leur sens, mais pour les priver de force, vertu et sagesse, par le moyen de ces jausnes et infernales lamies,

[1] The Sources of *Hamlet:* With Essay on the legend by Israel Gollancz. London 1926. pp. 109–111

49

produites par leurs serviteurs, ministres de corruption. Le pauvre Prince eust esté en danger de succomber à cest assault, si un Gentil-homme, qui (. . .) avoit esté nourry avec luy (. . .) avec certains signes fait entendre à Amleth en quel peril est ce qu'il se mettroit si en sorte aucune il obeissoit, aux mignardes caresses, et mignotises de la Damoyselle, envoyee par son oncle: ce que 'stonant le Prince esmeu de la beauté de la fille, fut par elle asseuré encor de la trahison: car elle l'aymoit dès son enfance, et eust esté bien mar(r)ie de son desastre et fortune, et plus de sortir de ses mains, sans jouyr de celui qu'elle aimoit plus que soymesme. Ayant le jeune seigneur trompé les courtisans et la fille soustenans qu'il ne s'estoit avancé en sorte aucune à la violer quoy qu'il dict du contraire, chacun s'asseura que véritablement il estoit insensé."[1]

There are between these two versions a number of common elements, which it may be convenient to describe giving their characters the same names as in Shakespeare's play with the German prefix Ur–

1. Ur–Hamlet, by his behaviour arouses the suspicion that he is all too sane and shrewd under his mask of folly.

2. Ur–Claudius, on the advice of a courtier (Ur–Polonius) decides to test him by tempting him with a woman.

3. This Ur–Ophelia is on familiar terms with Ur–Hamlet, with whom she grew up in the same environment.

4. Their meeting is observed.

5. He is warned of danger by Ur–Horatio.

6. He nevertheless does not give up his pleasure, and taking Ur–Ophelia out of sight of his 'lawful espials' ravishes her.

7. She is by no means unwilling and even in Belleforest loves him.

8. He enjoins her complete silence.

9. He declares to all that he raped her.

10. She, on his instructions, denies it.

[1] *Loc. cit.*, pp. 198–202.

Such is the material which Shakespeare had at his disposal for his own design. How did Shakespeare rearrange this material? Items one, two, three and four are just taken over. But we can observe at once a number of transferences: for instance, the spying scene (which in the similar case of the Queen's bedroom scene was lifted intact from Belleforest) is here transferred both in space and in spirit, from an impenetrable fen to the lobby in the castle; and from watching a regular attempt on Hamlet's virtue to eavesdropping at a meeting between two lovers or believed to be so. In both sources, Ur–Horatio warns Hamlet that his meeting with Ur–Ophelia is under observation. In *Hamlet*, Horatio is not available; but this tradition should be considered as a strong reinforcement for Dr. Dover Wilson's view that Hamlet himself overhears the plot beforehand; for this would be in harmony with the general relations between Shakespeare's play and its two sources.

All this warrants the assumption that Shakespeare took over also the chief feature of the Ur–episode: *Hamlet and Ophelia are in intimate relations.*

Before confirming this assumption with Shakespeare's own text, three reasons must be stated why it is most likely to be correct:

The first is that *Hamlet* takes its chief elements from Belleforest and Saxo Grammaticus with so much fidelity that the onus of the proof should really lie on those who deny rather than on those who assert that a particular feature has not been lifted. The only exception is that of details too crude or too unwieldy to be usefully incorporated on the Elizabethan stage; such as the fact that Ur–Hamlet carves and boils the body of Ur–Polonius before coming back to carry on his interview with his mother.

The second reason is that such a relationship would be more comprehensible and normal to an Eliazbethan audience than the Jane-Austenish coloured lithograph the nineteenth century has made of the episode. Indeed, it would be so normal to them that this may well be the reason why

Shakespeare did not make it plainer, though as we shall see, he made it plain enough.

And the third is that the situation thus created adds so much depth to the drama and to the tragedy that it is well nigh incredible that Shakespeare could have cast away such splendid material. Indeed the text of his *Hamlet* is enough to show that had it not been supplied to him by his sources, he would have added it himself. The design of *Hamlet* is rich in parallel lines. Fortinbras and Laertes are like thirds and fifths to Hamlet's melody. How could Shakespeare fail to see that by making Ophelia Hamlet's mistress he drew a parallel to the Claudius–Gertrude design and made Hamlet's tragedy twice as deep?

CHAPTER III

HAMLET AND OPHELIA :

SHAKESPEARE'S OWN WORDS

§ 1.   *The Sullied Flesh.*

The meaning of Hamlet's first soliloquy has been made clear by Dr. Dover Wilson's comment.[1] He rightly sees in it a pained meditation on the Queen's incestuous marriage; and by restoring the original punctuation, he has brought out the importance which Shakespeare meant his hearers to attach to this fact in itself, even before they had received any revelation or hint of the Queen's adultery and Claudius' crime.

Not the least of Dr. Dover Wilson's arguments is his emendation of 'too too solid' into 'too too sullied' in the first line of this soliloquy. But it is possible to accept this emendation, and even to add one or two arguments in favour of it, without altogether adopting the meaning and intention Dr. Dover Wilson lends to the word. In his view, Hamlet has in mind—or in heart—the stain cast on his flesh by his mother's incest. Now this reaction would be far from typical in as self-centred a type as we know by now Hamlet to be. The egotist feels no solidarity with any one, not even with his mother. He may *think* such a solidarity; he will never *feel* it. Hamlet here is *feeling*, as his passionate repetition of *too* shows. Therefore he cannot be feeling his mother's incest. The stain he laments cannot be as indirect as that. The thought of his mother's incest does focus and colour *the whole meditation;* but when he turns to his own 'too too sullied flesh', it is his own stain he is feeling.

This conclusion, based on Hamlet's character, is borne out by the very word Shakespeare here uses. After all,

[1] D. W. P., 39 ss.

Hamlet is a creature of Shakespeare; and where we say "Hamlet thought this", "felt that", we mean that Shakespeare wrote so as to make us think that Hamlet thought this or felt that. Now the word "sully" is used again by Shakespeare in Polonius' scene with Reynaldo: in a definite relation with pranks and vices committed by the young man himself:

You laying these slight sullies on my son,
As 'twere a thing a little soil'd i'the working.

Here, the word seems to have lingered in Shakespeare's mind from the first soliloquy. But what was it that brought it into the soliloquy? Hamlet, brooding on his mother's incest, feels a kind of disgust with the flesh in general; turns upon himself, *remembers his own secret intimacy with Ophelia*, and says:

O that this too too sullied flesh would melt!

Wherefore did "sullied" come into his mind? (Whose mind? Shakespeare's of course). The answer is plain: from Belleforest: *Ainsi furent deputez quelques courtisans, pour mener le Prince en quelque lieu escarté, dans le boys, et lesquels luy presentassent ceste femme, l'incitans à se souiller en ses baysers et embrassemens.* This is the origin of the word "sully", *souiller;* a definite allusion to Ophelia's kisses and embracements. That is what was in the mind of Shakespeare —Hamlet (one single mind, at the time he wrote), when the word 'sullied' came to his pen. Hamlet was then still in Shakespeare's being; and though the use of that word was premature *for the audience*, it was not so for Shakespeare, who, full of Belleforest's story, was conscious of the relations between Hamlet and Ophelia. The contemplation of Gertrude's incest was bound to cause in that part of Shakespeare's mind which he was then lending Hamlet, a painful resonance of his own "sully". That is why he repeats *too too* so ruefully; a repetition which conveys a self-reproach his mother's incest could not have justified. That is why Hamlet, at the thought of his mother's incest, feels that he wants his own flesh to melt, and why he feels "all the uses of the world stale, flat and unprofitable". Because his mother's incest makes him feel his own 'sullies' keenly; for were there no 'sullies' in him, he, Hamlet, self-centred as he was, would have remained untouched by his mother's stain, outside and above it, a judge, a critic, but never a victim of it.[1]

§ 2. *Hamlet's Sensuality.*

This wistfulness with which Hamlet rues his sullied flesh should not however be misunderstood so as to idealise him unduly. Hamlet is by no means that delicate soul, painted by romantic critics, who would sigh his pure and lily-white love under the window of his beloved and admired lady. He is a rather full-blooded and foul-mouthed man, whose natural bent in man-and-woman matters is particularly prone to carnal imagination. It is but a pious effort of his idolisers that tries to put the blame for his strong language on the situations, on his madness, and what not. The fact is that whether in a light and airy conversation with Rosencrantz and Guildenstern, or discussing his case with Horatio, or when pouring sarcasm on Polonius, or when angry with Ophelia, or when jesting at and through her, or when abjuring his mother to abstain from incestuous pleasures, or when warning her against letting out his secret, in every kind of occasion and with every kind of person, Hamlet is prone to revel in the coarsest and grossest language fit only for the barracks or the brothel. This is so strong a feature in the character that even when, alone, he is reproaching himself for his weakness, he breaks into unclean language "as to the manner born".

> Why, what an ass am I! This is most brave,
> That I, the son of a dear father murder'd,
> Prompted to my revenge by heaven and hell,
> Must, like a shrew, unpack my heart with words,

[1] True the word is used also by Belleforest in relation to Ur–Claudius: avant que mettre la main sanguinolente, et parricide sur son frère, il avoit incestueusement souillé la couche fraternelle. . . . The argument, however, remains intact. In the first example, *se souiller* touches Hamlet direct. Here it refers to the "couch", the married life of his parents; a 'sully' with an indirect effect on him.

> And fall a-cursing, like a very drab,
> A stallion![1]
> Fie upon't! foh!

Think of the experience of the unsavoury side of life
these words reveal; and bear in mind the details he dares
mention even to his mother:

> Let the bloat king tempt you again to bed;
> Pinch wanton on your cheek; call you his mouse;
> And let him, for a pair of reechy kisses,
> Or paddling in your neck with his damn'd fingers,
> Make you to ravel all this matter out,
> That I essentially am not in madness,
> But mad in craft.

and again:

> Nay, but to live
> In the rank sweat of an enseaméd bed
> Stewed in corruption, honeying and making love
> Over the nasty sty——

This was the imagination, this the inner world which
such critics as Bradley present as endowed with an exquisite
sensibility. The idea is preposterous. Hamlet was meant by
Shakespeare to be a strong, healthy man, drawn to women by
his carnal rather than by his spiritual side, and by no means a
merely romantic lover. And this feature of the character,
far too forgotten or neglected by actors and critics, should
be given the primordial importance it must take on when
dealing with his relationship with Ophelia.

§ 3. *Sermons to Ophelia.*

It so happens that the theme of Ophelia's virtue is the one
Shakespeare puts before the audience as soon as she appears
on the stage. Laertes first, Polonius later, speak of nothing
else to their sister and daughter; which shows that both are
uneasy about it. Shakespeare's intention is therefore clear.
He intends the audience to understand that Ophelia is free
enough with her favours to disquiet her father and brother.

[1] i.e. a brothel male prostitute.

Laertes is quite frank about what he fears; and he plunges into the subject when Ophelia has only said her first four words in the play. As for her attitude, it is meant to be sly and ironical throughout. Thus after all Laertes says to whittle down Hamlet's "favour", comparing it to:

> The perfume and suppliance of a minute,
> No more,

who cannot feel the suppressed mirth and mischievousness of Ophelia's answer: "No more but so?". As shown above, her second retort, sending back the ball of advice to her brother's side of the court, is meant as a hint to the audience on what it is she means by love.

As for Polonius, Shakespeare's hints to the audience through him could not be broader:

> 'Tis told me, he hath very oft of late
> Given private time to you, and you yourself
> Have of your audience been most free and
>   bounteous.

This is clear enough. But Shakespeare makes the old man drop yet another hint:

> If it be so—as so 'tis put on me
> And that in way of caution

And, in case the audience were in doubt, he makes Polonius say on:

> I must tell you
> You do not understand yourself so clearly
> As it behoves my daughter and your honour.

There is the word—honour—to make plain what the situation was. And so, rightly does Polonius end with a question:

> What is between you? Give me up the truth.

She hedges and parries with half confessions; just skilful enough to hide the facts from Polonius, but not from the audience, since this would not have suited the author. Thus, for Polonius:

> My Lord, he hath importuned me with love
> In honourable fashion.

And for the audience:

> And hath given countenance to his speech, my Lord
> With almost all the holy vows of heaven.

An Elizabethian audience was bound to feel that a young man in Hamlet's position need not swear to heaven that he loved a girl in Ophelia's position to marry her. All he need do is to inform her father. Since he swore so hard, the audience were bound to feel, he was getting something for his oaths, "mere implorators of unholy suits" as Polonius rightly comments. And when her father commands that she 'be something scanter of her maiden presence', her instant acquiesence shows she is dissembling; for where is the true love that would not have resisted such a stern command? And what are we to think of the innocence of a young lady, who, to all the rather insulting warnings of her brother and father, does not oppose a single word of protest? For, after all, if Ophelia had been what, so far, she is believed to have been, she would have broken in at the first hint from Laertes or Polonius and asked "What do you take me for?" Her long silences prove that she knew the sermons were but too justified.

Apart, however, from any of these questions of character, one of construction must here be faced: why these two scenes here? Why, at the moment an author is unfolding his play, when he needs every minute so that his statement of the facts does not weigh too heavily on the action, why bring in two successive and repetitious sermons on Ophelia's virtue and the risks she runs by having "private time" with Hamlet? And what could this "private time" be for between a girl of no particular intellectual powers and a young man as bent on sensual thoughts as his language shows throughout the play? Why tell us that Polonius has been warned by all and sundry that Ophelia might behave better "as it behoved my daughter and your honour?" Was Shakespeare likely to waste all this time on a theme which he did not think indispensable to "plant" in the mind of his audience precisely at this stage? Evidently not. We are now to see that for Shakespeare it was essential that his audience should know that Hamlet and Ophelia had strayed into intimacy without much depth of love before the Ghost came to invest the young Prince's life with a new and terrible meaning.

§ 4.   The Closet Scene.

The next thing that happens to Hamlet is the revelation that his mother had committed adultery with Claudius who, led by both desire of woman and ambition, had killed King Hamlet. The study of the full import of this revelation must be left for a later page. Here must be noted Hamlet's exclamation:

O most pernicious woman!

a guide to his thoughts. Before these thoughts emerge dramatically, Shakespeare places another scene, the first of the second act, in which Polonius instructs Reynaldo how to find out the kind of life Laertes is living in France. Here again Shakespeare leads the mind of his audience to sexual associations:

Drabbing—you may go so far.

and:

'I saw him enter such a house of sale'
Videlicet, a brothel. . . .

It is on this background that the great scene between Hamlet and Ophelia, which Shakespeare describes in Ophelia's words, is brought before the audience. It is evident that in this scene Hamlet is in deep distress; that he is not feigning; and that he has not yet the slightest reason for suspecting Ophelia, as he will later, of being ready to play the part of a decoy. No explanation has been provided for this scene; for, with all respect, Dr. Dover Wilson's is not an explanation at all. For him it is Hamlet's poignant appeal for help from the woman he loves. It is nothing of the kind. If Hamlet had really loved Ophelia, the scene would be unthinkable. He would have spoken to relieve *her* distress. Shakespeare made Hamlet's state of mind quite clear: the Prince came puzzled, distressed by

some kind of tense enigma the solution of which was in
Ophelia's face:

> He took me by the wrist, and held me hard,
> Then goes he to the length of all his arm,
> And with his other hand thus o'er his brow,
> He falls to such perusal of my face
> As a'would draw it. Long stayed he so,
> At last, a little shaking of mine arm,
> And thrice his head thus waving up and down,
> He raised a sigh so piteous and profound
> As it did seem to shatter all his bulk,
> And end his being; that done, he lets me go,
> And with his head over his shoulder turned
> He seemed to find his way without his eyes,
> For out adoors he went without their helps,
> And to the last bended their light on me.

The explanation of this scene is evident; but it requires
acceptance of two facts: Hamlet and Ophelia are in intimate
relations; and neither of them really knows what true love
is, Hamlet in particular being so self-centred that in this as
in every other scene of the play, he is thinking and feeling
only about himself.

The sequence of the facts is as follows:

(a) Hamlet and Ophelia had been "lovers" for some
time before the play begins;

(b) Hamlet is shocked by his mother's adultery, and
still more so by Claudius' crime as a consequence
of it;

(c) As time goes by, he is struck by the danger for
any man of becoming the toy of a woman he is
"interested in". Suddenly he turns the thought
upon himself; and this, as always, touches him
on the raw and leads to sudden and unbalanced
action. He thinks "what if Ophelia had only
consented in order to take me for her tool?"

(d) That is the enigma which Hamlet was trying to
read on her face. "Are you playing with me?"

This is a clear explanation, the only one which fits with the character of Hamlet and the facts which have occurred so far. We shall see it confirmed by later scenes.

Ophelia's haste in coming to tell her father is a masterly stroke. Hamlet's sudden visit has broken—or at least, so she may fear—the secret link between the two. She feels her solitude. She rushes to her father to make sure all is well there and that at any rate, with him, she has nothing to fear. It is a blind, instinctive move towards safety.

§ 5.   The ' Fishmonger ' Scene.

The next episode is the scene (II.2) where Polonius reads Hamlet's letter (a document of boredom and flippancy), and describes Hamlet as mad of love (which at different moments both the King and the Queen expressly say they do not believe). And then, the 'fishmonger' scene. No amount of ingenuity will enable critics who believe that Hamlet loved Ophelia to argue away this scene. True, Hamlet has overheard that Ophelia is to be used as a decoy; true, Polonius' words are highly provocative:

At such a time I'll loose my daughter to him.

But, in the generally accepted view, Ophelia is still innocent in Hamlet's eyes; and even if his mother's adultery has made him suspicious of women in general, and even if his love was brittle beyond compare, how could he, because another woman had failed, allow himself such obscene language not merely against his beloved's father but against his beloved herself? This explanation will not do. Indeed no explanation will make this scene intelligible at all that does not start from the fact that Hamlet had enjoyed Ophelia's favours.

The reason why Polonius' foolish line

At such a time I'll loose my daughter to him

provokes such a cataract of obscenities from Hamlet is because he harks back to his doubts, to that enigma he had vainly tried to solve by perusing Ophelia's face: "Why, my suspicions were only too well founded. Ophelia had been let loose on me. When I thought I was enjoying myself, I was being used as a tool by this old fool and his scheming daughter". That is what Hamlet is thinking when he calls Polonius 'fishmonger' and advises him not to let his daughter walk in the sun for "conception is a blessing; but as your daughter may conceive—friend, look to't". The 'fishmonger' scene cannot be adequately understood without referring it to that anguished scrutiny of Ophelia's face, nor this anguished scrutiny without that pre-existing secret intimacy between Hamlet and Ophelia which Laertes' and Polonius' sermons were meant to suggest.

Thus the sequence of scenes bearing on Ophelia are to develop logically in a deliberate design carefully drawn by the author.

§ 6.   The 'Nunnery' Scene.

Let us in passing note that this mood still lingers on when in the following scene, talking with Rosencrantz and Guildenstern, Hamlet banters about Fortune and her favours in a frivolous, cynical and obscene style; while Shakespeare drops yet another hint to the audience. "Man delights not me; no, nor woman neither, though by your smiling you seem to say so". The Court knows all about himself and Ophelia, or at least, so he suspects on seeing his friends smile. The Jephthah bantering and verses hark back to the same idea, the sacrifice of a daughter. And so through scenes which, though important for the general plot, add nothing to the theme of Ophelia, we come to the 'nunnery' scene. It begins with the great soliloquy on "to be or not to be", on which one word may be said here, with regard to those "pangs of despised love". Many critics have taken them as a cue for the deep suffering Hamlet is supposed to have undergone when Ophelia "jilted" him. But we know that Ophelia did not do such a thing, and that, even if she had, it would have left Hamlet pretty indifferent. Moreover, Shakespeare's text is as clear as day. Hamlet is wondering who would live on if the fear of what may happen in after life did not make people prefer the ills we have; and he enumerates them. Here they are:

> The whips and scorns of time,
> The oppressor's wrong, the proud man's contumely,
> The pangs of despised love, the law's delay,
> The insolence of office, and the spurns
> That patient merit of the unworthy takes.

Read the list again; keep out for the present the pangs of despised love; and ask yourself which of these 'ills' Hamlet could have experienced at first hand, he, the prince, heir to a kingdom. Shakespeare could not have conveyed more clearly that Hamlet had had no experience whatsoever of despised love than by putting its pangs on a list including the law's delay, the insolence of office and such other 'ills' Hamlet could not possibly have suffered. Hamlet is here speaking in general terms.[1]

And suddenly he sees Ophelia. She is reading. The tradition of making her kneel is a mistake. Polonius conveys Shakespeare's intentions:

> Ophelia, walk you here. Read on this book.

There is no reason whatever why she should be kneeling. A girl reading, particularly when walking, might be presumed to be reading a book of hours, the more so if, as is the case here, the observer is mischievous and ironic. Hamlet attacks at once. He has his background of fast flirtation to go upon. So, he says to himself:

> Soft you now!
> The fair Ophelia!

And to her:

> Nymph, in thy orisons
> Be all my sins remembered.

How did he know she was praying? it is asked. What did he care? Think of the fun of assuming that Ophelia, who for all he knew was reading a story such as Belleforest's, was actually muttering her "hours"; and of the irony of calling her *Nymph* so as to give a definite point and even a sting

---

[1] This was clearly seen by Bradley, pp. 156–7 fr.

to that "be all my sins remembered"; for didn't she know
them as closely as he?

Then begins a part of the scene which should be played
on such a spot of the stage and with such a voice on Ophelia's
part as to convey to the audience that the 'lawful espials'
cannot hear it, though they can, if they but peep, see the
gestures. For if Ophelia's

How does your honour for this many a day?
might pass off as suggesting to Polonius that the two had
not seen each other for many a day owing to Ophelia's
obedience to his orders, the reproaches Ophelia makes when
giving back the Prince's presents prove what her true
meaning was. The gesture would please her father; the
words by no means. There should be therefore in this scene
a definite difference in volume between Ophelia's voice and
Hamlet's. She having much to hide from her father, speaks
in a low voice; he, having no one to spare, and wishing to
be overheard, should shout. This is confirmed later by
Polonius:

How now, Ophelia!
You need not tell us what Lord Hamlet said;
We heard it all.

Then comes that "Ha ha! are you honest?" Dr. Dover
Wilson's analysis here is a considerable improvement on the
tradition which explained this outburst by making Hamlet
discover that Polonius is behind the arras. But his premises
do not account for the full blast of Hamlet's outburst. The
very fact that Ophelia produces the trinkets makes him feel the
plot. She is there as a decoy. Till then, he had been superior
and sarcastic at her expense, as he was with everybody; now
he is angry; not because she is a decoy there, in that rather
innocent role; but because this part of a decoy is but a
symbol and a reminder of the other and far graver part as
decoy which (he fears) she may have been playing in his
life from that day on which he thought it was he who was
using her as an instrument of his pleasure; while (the
thought makes him mad) it was she—was it she?—who had

been using him as an instrument of her ambition or whatever it was she was using him for. Nothing less than this can justify his violence. Ophelia had dared commit that unpardonable sacrilege—to use for her own purposes an egocentric man, the sacrilege an egocentric man never can forgive.

In his outburst of temper, Hamlet reveals all this: "Ay truly, for the power of beauty will sooner transform honesty from what it is to a bawd. . . . " that is, "your beauty has made a bawd of your honesty by sullying me with your kisses and embraces. . . ." And again: "I did love you once", in which he is sincere, because he knew no other love than "that". And she: "Indeed, my Lord, you made me believe so", after which one guesses the "for otherwise, I should not have yielded to you". And he: "You should not have believed me", which is a concrete reference to an act of belief, with its consequence now deplored by both. And then: "I loved you not"; to which she answers: "I was the more deceived". Note *the more*. Whereupon comes that "Get thee to a nunnery" tirade, which for Elizabethan spectators meant: "Go to a brothel, where you belong"—a clear sign that, for Hamlet, Ophelia had led him astray by prostituting her body to him.

This is immediately followed by an access of self-accusation, for he feels his own responsibility in the pity of it all; but also because he is backing out of those vows of heaven, i.e. those promises of marriage he had made to her in his passion; he will presently come to that, and with an illuminating remark: "If thou dost marry, I'll give thee this plague for thy dowry—be thou as chaste as ice, as pure as snow, thou shalt not escape calumny; (. . .) or if thou wilt needs marry, marry a fool, for wise men know well enough what monsters you make of them: to a nunnery, go, and quickly too, farewell."

That such things could be said by a loving Hamlet to a loved, or even to a once-loved, Ophelia, merely to punish her for having acted as an innocent decoy in a legitimate enquiry on his state of mind, is simply out of the question. He sends her to a brothel for having tried to make a monster of him by her guiles, for having sullied his flesh with her kisses and embracements. His reproaches about her paintings, her jig, amble, lisp, are all the bitter resentment of a male caught by a female too clever for him; and his "I say we will have no more marriage", coming after "it hath made me mad", is a notice served to the girl he had rashly promised to marry that there can be no question of *his* marrying anyhow, now that he realises he has been made a fool of—and very nearly "a monster", by the girl he thought he was playing with. Then, with a transparent threat to Claudius, he closes again with his "to a nunnery, go".

How does she react? Is it possible that her lamentations may have been understood as the utterance of a lover in deep distress? Are her words the cry of a heart mortally wounded? Are they not rather like an obituary notice in *The Times?* Ophelia is formal, ceremonious, courtly, affected. She is not natural. Her little speech is delivered for the ears of the King and of her father. There are, however, in it two lines which deserve notice: one is

And I of ladies most deject and wretched.

Shakespeare–Ophelia, writing that line, dared not call herself a maid; some subconscious inhibition in Ophelia's mind, still inside Shakespeare's, guiding the hand that wrote, censored out 'maidens' and wrote 'ladies' instead— for Ophelia knew she was not a maid. The second line worth noticing is the last:

To have seen what I have seen, see what I see!

§ 7. *The Play Scene.*

Unlike most critics and the tradition which prevails since Kean and Lamb, the King concludes:

Love! his affections do not that way tend

and though Polonius is of the contrary opinion, it is evident that Shakespeare meant us to side with Claudius in this.

Whatever the past, Hamlet is now possessed by the morti-
fying feeling that he has been, or was to be, fooled by
Polonius using his daughter as a tool. Just as Claudius had
been turned into a murderer by love of Gertrude, so
Claudius and Polonius had—he fears—schemed to turn
him into an idle Prince, content with his fate at Court, by
means of Ophelia. Hence the "Jephthah" taunt (II.2), a
transparent allusion to Ophelia. Jephthah sacrified his
daughter to his cause, as Polonius sacrificed Ophelia to his.
Nor will it do to argue that Jephthah's daughter bewailed
her virginity; for, since Ophelia is not being slaughtered,
what else can she have lost to be spoken of as a sacrifice?
Hamlet here carries on the chain of thought "fishmonger"
—"loose"—and as letting loose Ophelia for an innocent
"here are my trinkets back" scene can on no account justify
his language, the obvious conclusion is that it must all be
read in relation to an experience of intimacy between the
two.

The conclusion is clinched by the conversation between
Hamlet and Ophelia during the play scene. It is now clear
how and why Hamlet allows himself so many verbal
liberties with Ophelia. It is also clear that this conversation
is not supposed to be overheard. Hamlet may be mad and
Ophelia may be fast; but decencies are decencies; and the
remarks of Hamlet would not have passed unchallenged
even at Claudius'—i.e. Elizabeth's or James's Court (with
all respect for the historical school, the argument that the
gathering is not a Court but a number of actors and actresses
dressed as courtiers to add to the illusion, carries no weight
whatever. The illusion consists in that actors and actresses
are in fact what they are dressed as, for the time they are on
the stage). Nearly every word Hamlet addresses to Ophelia
at this moment, has an obscene meaning and is said with
that disregard for the other person's feelings which is
typical of self-centred characters. Hamlet here uses Ophelia,
speaks to himself through Ophelia, as if she were a mere
object, a prop for his thoughts; a target for his sarcasms,

irony, resentment. While Ophelia, far from listening with the pained patience of a friend who realises that the Prince is mad, and from seeking to distract his mind and soothe him—a part fondly read into the text by idealising and idolising critics—accepts the sport and even encourages him by her coy remarks.

This scene, therefore, a stumbling-block for so many commentators who on the basis of a pure, if foolish, Ophelia, are shocked and offended by it, becomes clear, logical, even inevitable when the facts, as meant by Shakespeare, are restored.

§ 8. *The Scene of Ophelia's Madness.*

Ophelia's madness is such a stage success in itself that it is taken for granted. But the question is there: why does Ophelia lose her reason? Or, more exactly, why does Shakespeare make Ophelia go out of her mind? We must always return to the master creator carrying the premises of his characters to their (æsthetically) logical conclusions.

Now on the generally accepted reading of her character, there is no particular reason for Ophelia to go mad. She has lost her father at the hands of Hamlet—a dreadful tragedy for her, but one a grown-up woman can stand. She has also lost his love, but, as she "jilted" him first, the situation is balanced; it can be lamented, but it is not one which would unhinge a healthy mind. There was nothing in it to *force* Shakespeare to push Ophelia into that state when she ceases to be a character and becomes a 'picture' or a 'beast'.

While the generally accepted view holds the field, Ophelia's madness lacks force and conviction. This explains how a woman of such feminine and æsthetic sensibility as Katherine Mansfield could write: "The 'Mad Scene', if one looks at it with a cold eye, is really very poor. It depends entirely for its effect upon poor wispy Ophelia. The cardboard King and Queen are of course only lookers-on. They don't care a halfpenny. (. . .) And who can believe that a solitary violet withered when that silly fussy old pomposity died? And who can believe that Ophelia really loved him, and wasn't thankful to think how peaceful breakfast would be without preaching?"[1]

But on the basis of an intimate and secret relationship between Hamlet and Ophelia the situation of the wretched girl's soul becomes such as to make madness inevitable. Ophelia carries in her young heart a secret she can only bear when shared with Hamlet. The frequent references to her "sweetness" and innocence made by Laertes and by the Queen (though by no one else) are meant to emphasise the tension in Ophelia's soul between her secret self and the person she is supposed to be for others. Taken at their face value by hasty readers, they gave rise to the legend of the "sweet maid". But, in drama, character is defined by deeds, not by words; by third-party opinions least of all. Ophelia feels the lonelier by all that praise of her innocence. When Hamlet rudely breaks the companionship, she is left cut off from the world by her secret. She can still live because she feels that any day may bring about her 'release' by either a return of Hamlet to her or even by her own confession to her father. But her father is killed and Hamlet is sent to England. The pressure becomes unbearable, and she must tell all. Sane she cannot speak: insane she must become.

That is the meaning of Ophelia's madness which a general examination of the facts forces upon us, before we have read the actual scene, or heard what she says in it. We know in advance that Ophelia will lose her reason in order to unburthen her heart from the secret of her love affair with Hamlet; and, therefore, that the mystery must come out into the open precisely in this scene.

Now let us look at the stage and hear what she says. She begins on her usual formal, affected style: "Where is the beauteous majesty of Denmark?" already singling out the Queen, for a deep-lying reason which will presently

[1] Quoted by John Hampden, M.A., in his edition of Hamlet, Nelson series, p. 182.

become apparent; then at once utters the theme of love:

How should I your true love know
From another one?
By his cockle hat and staff
And his sandal shoon.

"While this kind of devotion was in favour", writes Warburton,[1] "love intrigues were carried on under this mark. Hence the old ballads and novels made pilgrimages the subjects of their plots." Then she swings back to her father, whose death is so vital a factor in her state, though not merely out of filial love. Then "they say the owl was a baker's daughter", a hint at a daughter who would not be charitable enough and was punished, and then "Pray you, let's have no words of this (her secret), but when they ask you what it means, say you this": and she sings the Valentine song

To-morrow is Saint Valentine's day,
All in the morning betime,
And I a maid at your window
To be your Valentine.
Then up he rose, and donned his clothes
And dupped the chamber door,
Let in the maid, that out a maid
Never departed more.

The secret is out. But she is not yet satisfied; not clean enough. So, here come the most significant words of the whole scene:

"Indeed, la, without an oath, I'll make an end on't." Words after which nothing less than a complete confession can be expected. Here it comes

By Gis and by Saint Charity
Alack and fie for shame!
Young men will do't, if they come to't,
By Cock, they are to blame.
Quoth she, Before you tumbled me,
You promised me to wed.

[1] See Furness, p. 330.

70

(He answers)

> So would I ha'done, by yonder sun,
> An thou hadst not come to my bed.

Now she has made a clean breast of it; and what are her first words after this confession? Listen: "I hope all will be well." What a revelation of her state of mind! "Now that I have spoken, perhaps I shall be able to live!"

This done, she returns to her formal, social self, with a pathetic touch of ambition:

> "Come my coach!—Good night, ladies!"

All we had anticipated has happened. Ophelia has revealed her secret, since it was precisely in order to reveal it that she broke and destroyed her 'threshold'. Then comes Laertes' irruption; and Ophelia's second scene. Why a second scene? To show a different Ophelia. The first was tense with her secret; the second is just like a lute broken and out of tune, on which the hand of reason can no longer play. She gives flowers round, to each his due. She offers Laertes rosemary for remembrance and pansies for thoughts (which the rash youth was badly in need of) and the King fennel for flattery and columbines, "an emblem of cuckol-dom on account of the horns of its nectaria"[1]—by which Shakespeare meant to give one other hint to the audience, after so many, as to the young lady's knowledge of the things of life. Then, rue to the Queen and to herself, with that "we"

> "we may call it herb of grace on Sundays"

which pairs them off in significant solidarity. Is this not clear enough? 'We both'—she seems to say—'made the same error and must swallow bitter tears for it. We both gave our bodies for selfish aims'. The 'difference' has usually been interpreted as between the Queen and herself. But it is more reasonable to deduce from the text that by "you" she meant "one"; or even "we". 'Those who do have to wear rue wear it as no other person wears any other flower.' That is surely what she means. Then she says:

[1] Furness, p. 347.

"There is a daisy" and leaves it at that. To which Henley adds this explanation from Greene:[1] "Next them grew the dissembling daisie, to warne such light-of-love wenches not to trust every faire promise that such amorous bachelors make them!" Here again, another hint thrown at the audience by Shakespeare, and then, with the thought of violets she returns to her father.[2]

§ 9. *Ophelia's Death and Funeral.*

The Queen, in her poetical description of Ophelia's death, re-states the theme of flowers; but with what a strange detail!

> Therewith fantastic garlands did she make
> Of crow-flowers, nettles, daisies, and long purples
> That liberal shepherds give a grosser name,
> But our cold maids do dead men's fingers call them.

Steevens[3] says of this flower, long purples, that "In Lyte's *Herbal*, 1578, its various names, too gross for repetition, are preserved". One of them is "the *rampant widow*". It is the *Orchis mascula*. Why should the Queen go into all this near-obscene digression while describing Ophelia's garland! Is it not clear that Shakespeare wanted to be sure his audience knew what he meant them to understand Ophelia's life had been up to the very last? What other value are we to give to *Shakespeare's* deliberate and insistent words if we do not accept that he meant to describe Ophelia to the very last under a kind of sexual obsession?

The elaborate description of this scene entrusted to the Queen by Shakespeare, may well have been rendered necessary in his eyes by his desire to make it clear that

---

[1] Furness, p. 348.

[2] In a footnote, Bradley (p. 165) condemns those critics who "after all the help given them in different ways by Goethe and Coleridge and Mrs. Jameson, still shake their heads over Ophelia's song, 'To-morrow is Saint Valentine's day'. Probably they are incurable, but they may be asked to consider that Shakespeare makes Desdemona 'as chaste as ice, as pure as snow', sing an old song containing the line,
  If I court moe women, you'll couch with moe men."
The argument is irrelevant. Bradley confesses that he has no satisfactory interpretation for the Hamlet–Ophelia relationship. "I am unable to arrive at a conviction as to the meaning of some of his (Hamlet's) words and deeds (towards Ophelia)". And none of the three commentators he mentions can provide a consistent explanation of this scene.

[3] Furness, p. 37.

Ophelia did not take her own life. This was the logical outcome of her confession. She broke herself in order to confess her secret and gain peace—and so she died broken but at peace with herself:

> As one incapable (i.e. unaware) of her own distress.

The moving words of Laertes and of the Queen are for a considerable part responsible for the sentimental deformation the character has undergone in the course of time:

> Lay her i'th earth
> And from her fair and unpolluted flesh
> May violets spring!

says Laertes; and the Queen:

> Sweets to the sweet.
> Farewell!
> I hoped thou shouldst have been my Hamlet's wife.
> I thought thy bride-bed to have decked, sweet maid.

But with unfailing art, Shakespeare places between these two utterances of sentiment, the cold surprise of Hamlet: "What, the fair Ophelia!" This 'fair', which he has already used in another occasion, formal and indifferent, underlines the coldness with which he learns the death of the young woman. It is really—so far—no concern of his, surprised, of course, though he be. Not till Laertes loudly curses him three times does he feel personally involved; not till then does he come forward and bursts forth into the extravagant contest of mere 'ranting' which he presents as love. But the quantity and quality of his love may be gauged at this: once buried, Ophelia is clean forgotten. Never again does she come to his thoughts or lips.

CHAPTER IV

THE QUEEN AND THE KING

§ 1. *The Queen.*

The relationship between Hamlet and his mother, the favourite subject of psychoanalysts and other fanciful commentators, is on the whole relatively simple. Gertrude is a plain sort of a woman, not so much feminine as a female; sensuous and motherly, but again motherly in a simple and primitive way. The King, referring to Hamlet, reveals to Laertes that "The Queen his mother lives almost by his looks" (IV.7); and we know that she does not hesitate to lie in order to cover her son, for she is evidently making up an unbelievable story when, after Polonius' death, she answers the King's "Where is he gone?" with:

> To draw apart the body he hath kill'd;
> O'er which his very madness, like some ore
> Among a mineral of metals base,
> Shows itself pure; he weeps for what is done.
> (IV.2).

Every word Hamlet says on or about Polonius' death belies this statement. It is a typical utterance of a protecting but unintelligent mother.

Hamlet, however, is neither protecting nor unintelligent; he is, on the contrary, a first-rate mind and an egotistic heart. He sees through his mother with a double objectivity: that of the keen intellect and that of the cold heart. Strange that an attempt should have been made to explain his case as an Oedipus complex. Hamlet does not love his mother, not even in the carnal way an extravagant theory would have us believe. He does not hate her either. He just *thinks* her.

From the first scene in which we see them together he speaks to her, as he does to everybody, in that sibylline tone which seems to say: "Never mind if you don't understand

74

me. I understand myself and that is all that matters". In other words he speaks to himself through her. And when speaking about her to third persons he also uses the oracular and paradoxical style no one *need* understand.

> *Guil.* The queen, your mother, in most great affliction of spirit, hath sent me to you.
>
> *Ham.* You are welcome.
>
> *Guil.* Nay, good my lord, this courtesy is not of the right breed. If it shall please you to make me a wholesome answer, I will do your mother's commandment; if not, your pardon and my return shall be the end of my business.
>
> *Ham.* Sir, I cannot.
>
> *Guil.* What, my lord?
>
> *Ham.* Make you a wholesome answer; my wit's diseased; but, sir, such answer as I can make, you shall command; or, rather, as you say, my mother; therefore no more, but to the matter; my mother, you say—
>
> *Ros.* Then thus she says: your behaviour hath struck her into amazement and admiration.
>
> *Ham.* O wonderful son, that can so astonish a mother! But is there no sequel at the heels of this mother's admiration? Impart.
>
> *Ros.* She desires to speak with you in her closet ere you go to bed.
>
> *Ham.* We shall obey, were she ten times our mother.

The most curious feature of this relationship is the outspoken and even coarse nature of the language Hamlet uses with Horatio, to himself, and even to his mother when referring to her sexual life. This feature has given rise to the crop of psycho-analytical theories of Hamlet based on the Oedipus complex. But we need not wander from Shakespeare as far away in space and time and spirit as Freud was to explain Hamlet and Gertrude. This kind of coarse and obscene language was, we know by now, natural to Hamlet whatever the situation and the interlocutor; and as for his mother, he was able to apply it to her, not because he loved her (if, as we are told, incestuously) but precisely for the opposite reason: because, being a self-centred mind and heart, he saw her as a mere object and felt distant enough to talk to her as he did to everybody else.

Hence the bedroom scene. In the only two lines he says still thinking Claudius dead, Hamlet plainly accuses his mother of having killed his father:

A bloody deed! almost as bad, good mother,
As kill a King, and marry with his brother.

Shakespeare makes him insist:

Queen: As kill a King?
Hamlet: —Ay, lady, 'twas my word.

and it is then that he lifts the arras and finds he has only killed Polonius. Henceforth, though the Queen asks him twice what her crime has been, he mentions the murder no more, and speaks only of her incest.

This is a curious point in the play. That the Queen was guilty of marrying Claudius with unseemly haste, we knew from the beginning, for Hamlet says so in his first soliloquy; that she had committed adultery before marrying him we know from the scene between Hamlet and the Ghost; but that she had "killed" her husband? What does Hamlet mean?

He cannot be thinking of direct murder because he knows from the Ghost that the murderer was Claudius. He *may* be thinking that the Queen had aided and abetted the murder; but this is most unlikely, for otherwise he would have referred to the fact in his later reproaches to his mother. So the only explanation left is this: When he utters these words, Hamlet believes the King dead. The Queen (so he thinks) accuses him of the murder. He feels attacked. He repels the attack. "What about *you;* have you not——?" And in his passionate defence, he oversteps the bounds of factual truth to express the deeper truth of passion, since Gertrude "killed" King Hamlet by betraying him before his death and by marrying the murderer after.

76

This explanation follows the text literally; and fits in with the egocentric, subjective character of Hamlet. It shows him as ever swift in reacting to danger or direct attack, and forcibly twisting the mere facts of outward reality to suit his inner requirements. It is to his inner requirements and not to his father's revenge that he is attending when tackling his mother in the bedroom scene. A number of passages have prepared the audience for his state of mind. The play scene, in particular, is full of them, beginning with his rebuff:

Queen: Come hither, my dear Hamlet, sit by me.
Hamlet: No, good mother, here's metal more attractive.
Then, his remark to Ophelia:

> What should a man do but be merry? for, look you how cheerfully my mother looks, and my father died within's two hours.

Then, his spiteful: *Wormwood, wormwood!* whereby he expresses his enjoyment of his mother's suffering at hearing the lines:

> A second time I kill my husband dead
> When second husband kisses me in bed;

and later, when the Player-Queen has sworn verbose fidelity to her husband and he exclaims: "If she should break it now!"; till at last he asks her direct: "Madam, how like you this play?" A question prompted by his desire to see her embarrassed and ashamed, since no objective elucidation can be expected from her answer so far as *she* is concerned.

All this reveals a resentment against his mother which might at first sight be interpreted as a direct consequence of his feelings as his father's son. But, as the rest of the story shows, the resentment is of another nature. An infallible instinct deeper than any deliberate plan guided Shakespeare to adopt—or take over—this device of the play within the play to illustrate the attitude of Hamlet towards his mother. Deep down, it is the attitude of the spectator towards the actor. She lived, if badly; while he allowed Claudius to steal a march on him, not as Coleridge imagined, because his

intellect inhibited him from action, but because action
requires an outgoing—and his was an in-coming heart.

This is the mood in which he goes to see his mother.
After the dramatic first part ending with Polonius' death,
Hamlet takes a harsh offensive, and sets about to wring his
mother's heart. His first words are an accusation against
her adultery and her incest; indirectly also a profession of
faith in marriage vows as both civil ("contraction") and
sacramental ("sweet religion") bonds. In this first speech
Hamlet happens to use an image which has often been
referred, or rather transferred to his relations with Ophelia.

> Such an act
> That blurs the grace and blush of modesty,
> Calls virtue hypocrite, takes off the rose
> From the fair forehead of an innocent love
> And sets a blister there.

Critic after critic, anxious to explain Hamlet's coarseness
towards Ophelia as the outcome of a phase of resentment
following one of pure and ardent love, have seized on the
words "takes off the rose from the fair forehead of an
innocent love and sets a blister there"; and, tearing them
from their context, have transferred them to the Hamlet-
Ophelia episode (as understood by them). There is no basis
whatever for such a surgical operation. Hamlet is speaking
generally. He does not refer to any particular act. He is
enumerating. He is not even referring to the Queen's love
for her first husband. He is drawing a picture of the conse-
quences of acts such as that the Queen has committed; and
this picture is, indeed, so general that he calls the universe
to look on it with "tristful visage".

His picture, like everything he says, is highly subjective.
By no stretch of imagination can one see him here as the
incarnation of objective standards of morality. The accent
is not on society hurt or offended by un-ethical or un-
social acts; but on an ineffective Hamlet left high and dry
by the tide of life flowing past him. Of course, he accuses
the tide for carrying so much flotsam and jetsam of folly and

sin; but it is not really what it carries in its flow, it is the flow itself he resents.

That is why he soon passes on to a new line of attack, one in which ethical considerations are forgotten, and aesthetical feelings and standards hold the field. This is the long speech based on the parallel between the two portraits. Is there in all this sermon a single word to show that Hamlet would have objected to the Queen's "act" had Claudius looked like King Hamlet and King Hamlet like Claudius? And then the mounting rage and violence of his words, the coarseness which surges from his obscene underworld as soon as he comes near to that part of the Queen's "act" which recalls his own secret, his "too too sullied flesh"; to come out at last with what is, deep down, the true cause of his grief, temper, violence:

> A cutpurse of the empire and the rule,
> That from a shelf the precious diadem stole
> And put it in his pocket!

It is here that Shakespeare brings in the Ghost. King Hamlet, therefore, comes again, not to spare the Queen; not because, contrary to his commands, her son had not left her to heaven; but at the moment when the Prince, having emptied his bag of insults, shows bare the cause of his resentment—Claudius' success and his own failure. Shakespeare could not have been clearer. Hamlet himself provides the first clue:

> Do you not come your tardy son to chide,
> That, lapsed in time and passion, lets go by
> The important acting of your dread command?

and the Ghost confirms this guess easily made by the procrastinating Prince:

> Do not forget: this visitation
> Is but to whet thy almost blunted purpose.

Not a word about the Queen, so far. The purpose is blunted, that is why the Ghost came; not to defend the Queen. Then, with a significant *But*, he goes on:

> But, look, amazement on thy mother sits:

> O, step between her and her fighting soul:
> Conceit in weakest bodies strongest works:
> Speak to her, Hamlet.

No special significance, beyond a certain immediate dramatic effect, attaches to the fact that the Queen cannot see the Ghost; since the audience instinctively and without knowledge of any tradition thereon, must connect the fact with her adultery. To imagine that the Ghost steals away in shame on realising the cause of his opacity to her, is sheer romantic fancy.[1] The Ghost it was who had revealed her adultery to Hamlet, and as a true and well informed Ghost he must have known all the time that he would *therefore* be invisible for his faithless wife. This is our reasoning. Here is now a confirmation from the text: if the Ghost had any expectations of being seen by Gertrude, he must also have expected to be heard. Now, it is plain from his words to Hamlet that he entertained no such illusions; for otherwise, instead of requesting his son to speak to her, he would have spoken to her himself—and a most dramatic scene it might have been.

Nor is it possible to consider the middle phase of the scene as hallowed and blessed by the visitation. True, Hamlet feels chastened, and his coarseness is driven under, though not for long. But this short sermon to his mother is as self-centred and egotistic as everything else he says. He bids her confess and repent, and then come these amazing words:

> Forgive me this my virtue,
> For in the fatness of these pursy times
> Virtue itself of vice must pardon beg,
> Yea, curb and woo for leave to do him good.

This from the man who, on fearing he was being played with, but not before, had thrown Ophelia over. The undercurrent of self-revelation is continuous: the Queen says

> Hamlet, thou hast cleft my heart in twain;

and he promptly answers:

---

[1] Cf.: D.W., p. 255. He may, of course, mean that the Ghost just realises the reason why the Queen cannot see him, though the *fact* was known to him.

O, throw away the worser part of it,
(as he had thrown away that part which had played with
Ophelia)
And live the purer with the other half;
and then he goes on to explain how it can be done; did he
not know? Abstinence till it becomes a habit. Here Hamlet
is convinced that he has done right and that he is giving
his mother sound advice. But *what has all this to do with
avenging his father?* If he really means to kill Claudius, now
proved by the "play" to be his father's murderer, why urge
on the Queen the advantages of so time-taking a device
as *habit* in her relations with the King? Is it not evident that
all this talk, like his soliloquy on 'to be or not to be', is designed to show that Hamlet's procrastination is due to the
fact that his heart is not in his cause? The Ghost has just
reminded him that he is procrastinating; and he goes on to
display the finest piece of procrastination in the whole
tragedy.

This wandering from his purpose explains the savage
coarseness with which he returns to the theme of King
Claudius after his first leave-taking; and the fulsome
language of sexual images in which he casts it; then, once
this passion satisfied, he goes on to reveal to the Queen how
he plans to take action against Rosencrantz and Guildenstern during his voyage. Why this premature and, it would
seem, imprudent revelation? Simply because he is not really
talking *to* the Queen but to himself. This is shown by the
way he passes from the theme of his voyage to that of
Polonius' body, on which he says words of a detached
character, of a spectator, not an actor, of the drama of life.

§ 2. King Claudius.

A modern German commentator, referring to the King,
writes that "the parts of this figure are not modelled at one
cast, but so as to suit the action."[1] This, were it so, would

---

[1] So sind denn die Teile dieser Gestalt nicht aus einem Guss, sondern je nach ihrer Beteiligung an
der Handlung geformt—Schücking, p. 177.

invest with a new meaning the passionate words of Hamlet which bring back the Ghost: "A king of shreds and patches." Reasons for rejecting such a view can however be found on the very page in which it is put forward; for the argument that the character is incoherent because the man who could poison King Hamlet could feel no sympathy for Ophelia's sufferings, on which it is based, is one no person of experience can accept. The human soul is more many-branched and many-rooted than that. The King is in fact a strong and consistent character.

He stands in the play as the anti-Hamlet. We should not therefore take at their face value the opinions Hamlet expresses on him. When speaking of Claudius, Hamlet, in the Spanish saying, "breathes through his wound." He is hardly ever objective, but least of all when referring to his uncle; and this, be it remembered, even before he hears from the Ghost the revelation of his father's murder.

Claudius is the anti-Hamlet, not merely as Hamlet's natural adversary in the plot, but as his anti-type or anti-character. He is always on the spot. While Hamlet seems to absorb the play and drown it in his emotions, the King leads the events. He is the head of the State and he has usurped Hamlet's place; but the reasons are plain: he can lead and Hamlet can not.

His first speech is the most difficult. He has to pass over his access and marriage as over hot coals, and does so deftly, not without reminding his audience of Palatine Counsellors that they share his responsibility in the events; and, this done, he takes on the Norwegian affairs, Laertes, and finally Hamlet, with no faltering voice. He is ever clear, courteous, matter of fact, to the point. All in all, a masterful personality.

Shakespeare did not want his audience to believe that Hamlet's disparaging remarks on Claudius should be accepted as Gospel truth. The King, as directly expressed by Shakespeare, has dignity in every scene but those of intrigue with Laertes, and even then he manages to retain a certain kingly bearing. Shakespeare stresses his dignified attitude in the scene of Laertes' irruption, when he rejects the Queen's protection in truly royal words:

> Let him go, Gertrude, do not fear our person,
> There's such divinity doth hedge a king,
> That treason can but peep to what it would,
> Acts little of its will.

But this strong man has two weak spots. He is too fond of Gertrude and knows only too well how this fact unmans him: "she is so conjunctive to my life and soul," he says to Laertes; and he describes his attachment as "my virtue or my plague." His second weak spot is that, being a Borgian or Machiavellian, just like Hamlet, he is nevertheless tormented by a Christian conscience. Paradoxical as it may sound at first, Claudius the murderer is a better Christian than Hamlet who, indeed, is hardly a Christian at all. Shakespeare has emphasised this contrast time and again. In his soliloquies Hamlet reproaches himself for his inability to kill his uncle, unable to realise why he cannot bring himself to the deed. Not once does he raise the moral issue: "Have I a right to kill the King?" If that inhibition he cannot explain to himself (which we know to be an essential and primal indifference or lovelessness) did not stand in the way, he tells us what he would do:

> I should ha' fatted all the region kites
> With this slave's offal.

Qualms, he has none.

The King, on the other hand, is ever labouring under a Christian sense of sin and often, through the play, a word, a situation are enough to bring to the surface the undercurrent of guilt that flows in his dark soul. How adroitly suggested is this state of uneasiness in the two lines:

> He tells me, my dear Gertrude, he hath found
> The head and source of all your son's distemper.

We hear the unexpressed hope that it may be elsewhere than where the Queen at once and somewhat brutally puts it:

> I doubt it is no other but the main,
> His father's death and our o'erhasty marriage.

And again, when unconvinced by Polonius' assurance, he asks, "How may we try further?"; and before that, when, requesting Rosencrantz and Guildenstern to study Hamlet, he volunteers to say:

> What it should be,
> More than his father's death, that thus hath put him
> So much from th'understanding of himself,
> I cannot dream of;

these words "more than his father's death", are an involuntary release, a whiff of air for his locked up secret. Then come the pathetic words just before the 'nunnery' scene: "Read on this book," says Polonius to his daughter; and the old man moralising in an idle and general way, goes on:

> We are oft to blame in this,—
> 'Tis too much proved—that with devotion's visage
> And pious action we do sugar o'er
> The devil himself.

These words at once wake up the King's torment:

> O, 'tis too true!
> How smart a lash that speech doth give my con-
> science!
> The harlot's cheek beautied with plastering art,
> Is not more ugly to the thing that helps it
> Than is my deed to my most painted word:
> O heavy burthen!

Thus the voice of the King's conscience hints, suggests, speaks through the play till it bursts forth in: "Give me some light, away!", a cry from the heart logically unconnected with the situation, for there was no need of light despite Polonius' fussy "lights, lights, lights", but in strict obedience to a subconscious command: it was light the King's soul needed.[1]

The direct effect of this crisis is the 'prayer' scene. It provides Shakespeare with an opportunity for a soliloquy

---

[1] Cf. the powerful cry of the fisherwoman Tisbea in Tirso de Molina's masterpiece *El Burlador de Sevilla* when, suddenly realising Don Juan has betrayed her, breaks into the stage crying:

Fuego, fuego que me quemo,	Fire! Fire! I burn! I burn!
Que mi cabaña se abrasa.	My cottage is all ablaze!

in which the King reveals his inner thoughts. We then see patently that in the King's soul there is a conflict between desire and ambition on the one part and Christian contrition on the other, which is wholly alien to Hamlet. How different from Hamlet's soliloquies! Here, for the first time, we perceive the voice of deep human grief. Passionate, the soliloquies of Hamlet certainly are; but the despair of a soul at bay, the voice of a soul heavy with crime, longing for repentance, yet unable to repent, the poignancy of its appeal to divine mercy reach in this soliloquy a tension which none of Hamlet's soliloquies attain. And after Hamlet has come and gone the tortured King rises, giving a perfect matter-of-fact expression to his hopeless dilemma:

My words fly up, my thoughts remain below.
Words without thoughts never to heaven go.

His inner torments, however, do not prevent him from taking action. His style in the scene when the Queen comes in tears with the news of Polonius' death is prompt and executive. His plan is clear: to send Hamlet away and to remain outwardly calm towards the world:

The sun no sooner shall the mountains touch,
But we will ship him hence: and this vile deed
We must, with all our majesty and skill,
Both countenance and excuse. Ho, Guildenstern!

And in his scene with Hamlet, he does not allow the young man to unharness him with his gibes, taunts and verbal pranks.

He is upset, and in the company of his wife, is almost overcome by a wave of weakness when, just after Ophelia's mad scene, he has to tell the Queen about Laertes' return:

O, my dear Gertrude, this
Like to a murdering-piece in many places
Gives me superfluous death!

But the tumult ramming at his doors brings him back to his virile self and he soon masters the petulant young man. Then, on learning that Hamlet has returned, he plots the Borgian murder of Hamlet just as Hamlet had plotted that

of Rosencrantz and Guildenstern. Things turn out otherwise than he had meant, and in the end he is killed by Hamlet when he had lavished his blandishments and diplomacy
to trap Hamlet into death. But to the very end he remains
a man of initiative. Helpless when wounded, he tries to
retrieve the situation in his last words:

O, yet, defend me, friends, I am but hurt.

§ 3. The Mouse-Trap.

The play within the play presents a number of problems
to the interpreter of Shakespeare; one of them, that the
players should arrive in Elsinore with a play in their
repertory nearly identical with the secret tragedy of King
Claudius and King Hamlet. This, however, turns out to be
no problem at all. A coincidence? No doubt. But since, at
all times, drama has been written on crimes committed by
men, Shakespeare was by no means overstepping the boun-
daries of the believable in assuming that one of the many
plots the players knew by heart suited the secret facts about
King Hamlet's death.[1]

The actors know nothing about the way in which King
Hamlet died; they see therefore no reason why they should
not play that plot as such. Nevertheless, a formidable
objection does remain: how could the players dare stage a
play in which the Queen expatiates so heavily on the theme:

A second time I kill my husband dead

When second husband kisses me in bed?[2]

For, though they knew nothing about King Hamlet's
murder, they were fully aware of Gertrude's second marriage celebrated just two months before they spoke. This
circumstance should have been enough to make them step
back on Hamlet's suggestion that such a play should be
staged; and if few spectators of *Hamlet* are struck by the
situation, it cannot but shock the readers. The mouse-trap
is really impossible. It is a hastily contrived piece of stage-

---

[1] This much had to be said in view of D.W., pp. 141-3.

[2] Curiously enough, this difficulty is not touched upon by D.W. in his otherwise exhaustive study
of this subject.

craft; one like the several to be examined later in which Shakespeare reveals himself indifferent to certain niceties of his craft.

But the statement has to be carefully qualified. The contrivance is defective in that Shakespeare neglected to justify the players in some way or other, such as a bribe, an assurance of protection, some show of resistance on their part; for otherwise, the choice of the second marriage theme for the test play is admirable, since it draws the King's attention while in a certain sense putting him off the scent of what is coming. But here again this point, the attention of the King to the play which is to test him, raises the problem of the Dumb-Show. Why a dumb-show at all? Three answers to this question have been put forward: one, that the dumb-show is there to prove that the King did not murder King Hamlet; and that the Ghost was but Hamlet's hallucination. The second answer is that Claudius stands the dumb-show but is upset by its spoken reiteration. Both these answers are refuted by Claudius' uneasy question when watching the play: "Have you heard the argument? Is there no offense in't?"

The third answer[1] amounts to this: the "play" is hardly a play at all. It is a dialogue on second marriage followed by a brief incantation-and-poison episode which the King's scare cuts short. It was indispensable to inform the public of what was coming so that they could the better expect the discomfiture of the King. Hence the Dumb-Show, during which the King, whose mind is on other matters, talks with Polonius and the Queen and notices nothing.

But the necessity of the Dumb-Show is by no means proved thereby. The public know from the Ghost that King Hamlet had died from a poison poured into his ear; and from Hamlet that, in the play:

> One scene of it comes near the circumstance
> Which I have told thee of my father's death.

The Dumb-Show adds nothing to all this. The audience

---

[1] The two first answers are, I believe, well refuted by D.W. The third is his own—pp. 144 ss.

hear all about second marriages and about "none wed the second but who killed the first", and are ready for anything. The play is cut short but not till it has yielded all it was expected to yield both by Hamlet and by the audience, and the Dumb-Show is unnecessary.

Then, why the Dumb-Show? Because it was there, perhaps, in the Ur-plot, certainly in the tradition; and because, though useless, it could be turned to account by a good dramatist. It has been suggested that Hamlet watches it with some dismay lest it spoil his own plot; for though he would, of course, equally well test the King with a Dumb-Show as with the play, the Dumb-Show might fail to catch the Queen, whom he also wants to test. Hence, it is argued, his "miching mallecho, it means mischief", which would apply to the players and not to the King; as well as his "the players cannot keep counsel; they'll tell all".

The case is far from proved. The words *miching mallecho* remain as obscure as a number of Hamlet's utterances; but the most natural explanation of them is that Hamlet, answering Ophelia, is, as usual, talking to himself and describing to himself what he himself has planned and sees in his mind. "What means this, my Lord?"—asks Ophelia. And he, with those two words answers: "This is scheming in the dark; you just wait and see." The Dumb-Show is just one more phase in the tension and the excitement with which the audience watches for the King's crime to unkennel itself.

Those who hold that the speech inserted by Hamlet is the incantation, have not proved their case either. The strongest argument against them is precisely the Dumb-Show. Without it, we might argue that the play was not as like Claudius' murder as Hamlet wished, and that therefore the words uttered by Lucianus had to be inserted in order to make it so. But we know by the Dumb-Show that the poisoning-to-the-ear scene was there all the time; and we know it also from the words of Hamlet to Horatio:

One scene of it comes near the circumstance
Which I have told thee of my father's death.

It is therefore most unlikely that Hamlet should have granted so much importance to the terrific incantation, the style of which, by the way, is worthier of the "original" "knavish piece of work" than of the fastidious prince. Nor should we, as some do,[1] interpret the words:

> if his occulted guilt
> Do not itself unkennel in one speech

as referring to the dozen or sixteen lines Hamlet meant to insert; for "in" can convey no such meaning; "one" means "at least one", and "speech" means almost certainly "utterance" of the guilty King, since it is "in" that speech that the hidden guilt is expected to reveal itself.

All goes to show that Shakespeare did not attach much importance to that speech Hamlet had announced to the players, except perhaps as a contrivance to keep his audience taut, in wait for it. For, in fact, one of the marvels of *Hamlet* is that in it things happen by a logic of their own not always identical with the concatenation prearranged by the author. Hamlet contrives the play to show up (or test) his uncle's murder of his father; but, drawn by his own passionate nature, what he reveals is his own resentment and suspicion of his mother, and his hankering and unsatisfied desire to kill his uncle.

Hence his repeated remarks whenever a striking, clear line of verse reminds the Court of his mother's o'erhasty marriage and later that improvisation: "This is one Lucianus, nephew to the King"; and again: "Come: the croaking raven doth bellow for revenge"—a reminiscence from a passage in a play *The True Tragedy of Richard the Third*, full of the theme of revenge. With masterly hand Shakespeare turns the tables of the experiment. It is the tester who is most tested of all. His whole psychology being one of a spectator rather than an actor in life, he cannot repress his remarks as such. The attention of both the real and the stage audience is diverted to Hamlet from the King and Queen on whom Hamlet himself meant it to be concentrated. So that when

[1] e.g. Dowden, p. 112.

the King at last unkennels his guilt, what the Court sees is less a King unmasked by an astute and wronged son than a King threatened by a passionate and ambitious nephew.

This scene, therefore, owes much of its force to the life-like independence with which events in it seem to burst forth through and around the plans of the Prince and even of the Poet. The "speech", so carefully "planted" by Shakespeare and prepared by Hamlet, is not delivered at all. The King gives himself away, but Hamlet no less so; and the Court disperses in a confusion of diverging fears, a true image of life's own crises.

CHAPTER V

THE INNER TRAGEDY

§ 1.   *Hamlet's Unhappiness.*

The ground is now free for a study of Hamlet's real tragedy.
It is clear that the Prince is a thoroughly unhappy man.
The grief of his father's murder and the indirect humiliation
implied in his mother's marriage were terrible blows; but,
from the outset, Shakespeare manages to convey the
impression that, more even than the blows themselves,
what matters is the resonance they call out from the depth
of Hamlet's soul. Why is he unhappy? On the face of it, he
need not have been. True he is not the King, but he is the
heir, and, for a young and active man, the position might
have presented all the advantages of the Crown without
its drawbacks. Moreover, the two terrible events should
normally have excited his anger rather than depressed him
into a melancholy. A young, strong and courageous man
such as he was need not have taken his father's death in the
mournful way he does when addressing his mother in Act I:

Seems, madam! nay, it is; I know not "seems".
'Tis not alone my inky cloak, good mother,
Nor customary suits of solemn black,
Nor windy suspiration of forced breath,
No, nor the fruitful river in the eye,
Nor the dejected haviour of the visage,
Together with all forms, modes, shows of grief,
That can denote me truly; these indeed "seem",
For they are actions that a man might play;
But I have that within which passeth show;
These but the trappings and the suits of woe.

Nor can the explanation be accepted that would attribute
the mournful, instead of the manly, reaction to "weakness"
or to "mental infirmity"; since Hamlet was by no means
weak, and mental infirmity is no subject for a tragic author:

it belongs to the hospital. The only conclusion to be drawn from all this is that Hamlet was an unhappy man before he knew from the Ghost that his father had been murdered. True he knew of his mother's hasty marriage, but, for reasons to be given later, this fact cannot provide a suitable explanation for his unhappiness.

Furthermore, it is also plain from the outset that Hamlet is not the kind of man whose happiness or unhappiness depends on events outside his own being. In fact, what makes this play so haunting is that it really does not happen on the stage but within Hamlet's soul. We know by now how self-centred Hamlet is; but none of the observations of detail that have led us to stress this feature of his character illustrates it so well as this: that by sheer self-centredness Hamlet draws the whole tragedy to himself and makes it flow within the spacious halls of his melancholy soul.

The play is full of tragedies: that of King Hamlet, betrayed by his wife and murdered by his brother; that of Polonius, killed like a calf because he would "be too busy"; that of Rosencrantz and Guildenstern, sent to their doom by Hamlet himself undeservedly and unnecessarily; the moving tragedy of Ophelia; that of King Claudius, who won a crown but lost his peace; and lastly that of the Queen herself, a character in which the lower and the higher passions struggle without inner leadership. And yet, all these tragedies, nearly all of which would have provided a substantial chief theme for a whole play, is sunk into the one tragedy of the all-absorbing Prince. Where Hamlet suffers, no other suffering counts.

It follows that the golden rule for the right understanding of this play is to refer to Hamlet everything that happens in it.

§ 2. *Hamlet's Ambition.*

This is particularly the case with Hamlet's ambition and the passions it awakes in him. The butt of his remarks on this theme is, naturally enough, his uncle:

Does it not, think thee, stand me now upon
He that hath killed my King, and whored my
    mother,
Popped in between th'election and my hopes. . . .
                    (V.2).

he says to Horatio. And the word ambition is let out—somewhat rashly—by Rosencrantz in the very first dialogue he
crosses with the Prince:

Hamlet.   Denmark's a prison. (. . .)
Rosencr. Why, then your ambition makes it one:
            'tis too narrow for your mind.

The theme is embroidered by the three young men in a
manner which recalls the *concerto cadenzas* when the pianist
wanders away all over the keys, yet comes back in due time
to where the orchestra is patiently waiting for him:

Hamlet.   O God! I could be bounded in a nut shell,
            and count myself a King of infinite space;
            were it not that I have bad dreams.
Guil.   Which dreams, indeed, are ambition:
            for the very substance of the ambitious
            is merely the shadow of a dream.
Hamlet.   A dream itself is but a shadow.
Rosencr. Truly, and I hold ambition of so airy and
            light a quality, that it is but a shadow's
            shadow.
Hamlet.   Then are our beggars bodies, and our
            monarchs and outstretched heroes the
            beggars' shadows. . . .

As in a true *cadenza* the variations are free and "airy",
but the theme is heard again and again—"ambition" on
the lips of Hamlet's friends; and on his lips "*King* of
infinite space", "*monarchs* and outstretched heroes".

Though with as light a hand as even he ever let run on
the keyboard of language, Shakespeare here conveys this
aspect of Hamlet's tragedy to his audience. Later, when with
scant courtesy he receives the unfortunate Rosencrantz
sent by his mother after the 'mouse-trap' scene, the theme

of thwarted ambition is stated again with almost brutal
frankness:

Rosencrantz: Good my lord, what is your cause of dis-
temper? (. . .).

Hamlet: Sir, I lack advancement.

Rosencrantz: How can that be, when you have the voice
of the King himself for your succession in Denmark?

Hamlet: Ay, Sir, but 'while the grass grows'—the
proverb is something musty.

These passages provide the key to Hamlet's real state of
mind with regard to his ambition and his disappointed
hopes of being elected to the throne. They were mere
hopes, not *rights;* this is an important point. Every time the
throne vacated the new King had to be elected. Therefore,
Claudius had wronged young Hamlet twice: first by
murdering his father; and then by "popping in between the
election and his hopes". The usual conclusion is that Hamlet
felt this double grudge against Claudius: the King's
murderer and:

> A catpurse of the empire and the rule
> That from a shelf the precious diadem stole
> And put it in his pocket.

This, however, by no means exhausts the true relationship between Hamlet and Claudius. If it did, Hamlet
would be taking a far deeper interest in Claudius as Claudius,
than he could ever have taken in any human being. Both
in his soliloquies and in his objurgations to his mother,
Hamlet waxes eloquent on 'the murderer and the villain';
on the 'slave's offal':

> Bloody, bawdy villain!
> Remorseless, treacherous, lecherous, kindless villain!

But the very violence and coarseness to which the thought
of his uncle drives him shows that Hamlet is not pouring
forth moral indignation; nor even giving vent to what
might be described as his "objective passions", the reactions
of a bruised heart at the man who had killed his father and
whored his mother. Given his general character, his lofty

brain and heart, he would have reacted with a hotter and cleaner indignation. The coarse and violent language in which he pours forth his emotions confirms that, though he is *thinking* of his father and mother, he is feeling at a deeper level; as indeed he was bound to do, for, were it not so, again, Hamlet would be attaching more importance to his father and to his mother than to himself—an attitude out of all harmony with his self-centred nature.

This coarseness and this violence of Hamlet's attacks on Claudius are due to a wholly internal drama, to a desperate struggle which is tearing his soul to pieces. Neither his father killed, nor his mother estranged, nor his crown usurped matter for Hamlet, except as mere tokens of his defeat. What Claudius has done to him, the deepest wound and the agony which the name Claudius evokes in his aching soul is that while that "slave's offal" got to business and triumphed, he, Hamlet, went about like John-a-dreams, unpregnant of his true cause, which was, not to avenge his father, but to fulfil Hamlet's destinies.

That is the true tragedy of Hamlet: not his incapacity to avenge his father; not his frustrated ambition; but his incapacity to be Hamlet. He can think Hamlet; he cannot be Hamlet. The pathetic soliloquy which ends Act II.

O, what a rogue and peasant slave am I!
is the desperate comment of the unfortunate prince on this discovery. He attributes his own ineffectiveness to cowardice, which is of course a false scent; then gets into a passion; then realises how foolish he has been; then calls his brain to act; and finds calm in action by deciding to test the King with the play. Yet, beneath all this process of many moods, he again procrastinates; he again proves, in fact, unable to act. He has not discovered the root-cause of his ineffectiveness. He is to die without having discovered it.

§ 3. *Hamlet's Procrastination Unexplained.*

It is a striking fact in English Literary History that Hamlet's procrastination, the main spring of the play, has to this date remained, in the last resort, unexplained. Bradley made an excellent summary of the history of its interpretations. He discusses and, of course, rejects first the view that Hamlet was baulked by external difficulties such as the King's bodyguard; the absence of a better proof than a Ghost-story; the fact that when he had the King at his mercy, he could only have murdered him, which would not have been justice; and the swift action of the King when, back from the sea-voyage, Hamlet has at last a proof of the King's treachery. All this need not even be argued.

The next view discussed is that which would assign Hamlet's procrastination to moral scruples. It is easy to prove, text in hand, that this view is untenable, and Bradley does so admirably, particularly when he dismisses that aspect of the theory which attracts him most—that even if Hamlet admitted the moral right to kill his father's murderer, a "deep unconscious conscience" in him rebelled against the deed. Curiously enough, Bradley does not mention the strongest argument against the 'moral scruple' view—Hamlet's behaviour to Rosencrantz and Guildenstern, which shows him ready unnecessarily to sacrifice two human lives in a singularly callous manner.

Bradley then discusses the view of those who attribute Hamlet's procrastination to some aesthetic rather than moral repulsion. He quotes Goethe: "a lovely, pure and most moral nature, without the strength of nerve which forms a hero, sinks beneath a burden which it cannot bear and must not cast away." He refutes this view no less admirably than the two previous ones, recalling not only Hamlet's manliness, but even his hardness and cynicism and his insensibility towards Rosencrantz and Guildenstern. Note, however, that loaded with pro-Hamlet prejudice, or better, having preconceived Hamlet as "a soul so pure and noble", he is led to writing that this view "ignores the hardness and cynicism which were indeed no part of his nature, but yet, in this crisis of his life, are indubitably present and painfully marked." And again: "That this embitterment, callousness, grossness, should be induced on a soul so pure and noble is profoundly tragic"; passages in which Bradley, while rejecting what he calls "the sentimental view" falls into it himself.[1]

For what is it exactly he means by "they are indubitably present", referring to features of which he says that they were indeed no part of Hamlet's nature? And is it not obvious that the good, polished, modern British scholar is refusing to see the facts, and, not wholly unaware of this refusal, hedges and half-owns—out of sheer honesty—what —out of sentimental refinement—he does not want to see? Why are the 'hardness and cynicism which were indeed no part of his (Hamlet's) character' not only 'present' (come from where?) but 'painfully marked'? What 'pain' is this but that of adjusting the real Hamlet to the preconceived and inexistent Hamlet the polished scholar wanted Shakespeare to have conceived for him?

Finally, Bradley discusses the Schlegel-Coleridge view when he sees in Hamlet's procrastination 'the tragedy of reflection', more or less modified by Dowden's ideas on the influence of the emotions. With his usual acumen, Bradley, having granted that the theory is in excellent harmony with the text, owns that it 'fails to satisfy'. But in marshalling his arguments against it, as well as in presenting his own view, he is handicapped by his own sentimental prejudices. Briefly put, his theory rests on the following ideas:

1.—Hamlet was not naturally or normally but only circumstantially unable to carry out the task laid on him by the Ghost.

2.—He was of a melancholic temperament, i.e. inclined to nervous instability, to rapid and perhaps extreme changes of feeling and mood.

3.—He was a man of "exquisite sensibility to which we may give the name 'moral', if that word is taken in the wide meaning it ought to bear". In this lay the danger of tragedy if his sensibility came to be *shocked*.

[1] Bradley pp. 104, 103.

4.—He was a man of intellectual genius. This, however, implied no danger, for "the idea that the gift and the habit of meditative and speculative thought tend to produce irresolution in the affairs of life would be found by no means easy to verify." Yet, were his moral sensibility shocked, action being denied to him, his imagination would increase his melancholy.

This is, according to Bradley, what actually happens. And the shock came from his mother's behaviour, as he describes it in the first soliloquy.

Now this interpretation requires first a sentimental idealisation of Hamlet's moral sensibility which his behaviour towards everybody in the play makes unacceptable. The Hamlet who sends Ophelia to a nunnery, and pokes obscene fun at her, the man who called Polonius "fishmonger" and all the rest of it, the man who contrives the murder of Rosencrantz and Guildenstern, could not be described as of such a moral sensibility as to be sunk in paralysed melancholy because his mother committed adultery and remarried. And if his melancholy prevents him from killing his uncle, why does it not stand in his way when he kills Polonius and boards the pirate ship and sends Rosencrantz and Guildenstern to their doom and swears he will make a ghost of anyone who stops him from seeking the Ghost? Bradley has to assume that Hamlet had "morbidly" centred his sensibility in but one action only, the one for which he felt unequal. This is begging the question. Bradley's interpretation explains nothing.[1]

§ 4. Hamlet's Procrastination Explained.

We must revert to the view Bradley rejected and take it that Hamlet was not circumstantially but naturally and normally unable to perform the task laid on him by his father. This is, so far, of course, a working hypothesis which has to be

[1] 109 et seq. I do not discuss Dr. Dover Wilson's views because they rest on 'mental infirmity' and on 'we were never intended to reach the heart of the mystery', p. 229. I need not argue either the case that there is no procrastination (cf. Stoll, H., p. 51, Schücking, 216) for it is untenable. The argument that the reasons given by Hamlet not to kill the King at prayers are cogent is irrelevant. For the man who wants to procrastinate, cogent arguments are more valuable than mere pretexts.

proved correct. A true interpretation of Hamlet's procrastination must fit in with the text, with the character, and with
the facts.

Now, there are two facts which rule the whole issue:
the first is that Hamlet cannot bring himself to kill Claudius;
the second is that he kills him twice (first, in intention,
when he kills Polonius; then, at the end of the play). An
examination of this contrast will provide us with the key
to the mystery.

No time need be wasted as to the first, or negative aspect
of the question. It is now common ground that the soliloquies and other utterances in which Hamlet puts forward
reasons for adjourning his vengeance are but sublimations
of his inability to act. What remains still to be explained is
the reason for this inability. Now the best way to find out
why he does not kill when he doesn't is to find out why he
kills when he does.

The first time Hamlet kills the King is when he slays
Polonius behind the arras. Let the circumstances be considered. Hamlet has vehement suspicions, bordering on
proof, that Claudius has murdered his father. Two factors
only stand between his suspicion and his conviction: doubt
as to whether the Ghost was genuine, and his own subconscious desire to disbelieve, so that no action be necessary.
Then comes the play. Hamlet is convinced. His uncle *is* a
murderer. Yes; but the 'mouse-trap' has yielded a second
result: *Claudius knows that Hamlet knows.* What is the
obvious conclusion for Hamlet? "Now is my turn." From
the moment the King "unkennels" his secret to Hamlet,
the play turns into a sharp duel of wits. Hamlet is in danger.

In his first exhilarated mood, Hamlet does not realise
all this. Self-centred, as usual, he does not see the reactions
of others to his moves. He passes by the spot where the
King is praying and lets the opportunity go by to get rid
of his enemy; but when in the Queen's closet, he hears a
noise behind the arras, in the jumpy atmosphere created by
the Queen's own fears, Hamlet feels the immediate threat

to his own person. That is why his suspicions settle on the King and the idea that Polonius might be there does not come to his mind. The chain of inner reactions would be: "hiding, treachery, crime, threat to me, King." Then Hamlet does not hesitate. He kills the King.

"The King" he has killed turns out to be Polonius. But that is a purely external fact, and as such, does not interest him overmuch. This is one, possibly the chief, reason for the callous way in which he makes the discovery. For Hamlet the world is divided into two parts: beyond his skin, world of little importance; within his skin, world of capital importance. Beyond his skin Hamlet has killed Polonius, a detail of little weight; within his skin, he has killed the King; hence his serenity, for the King deserved his fate.

All this applies to the scene of Claudius' actual death. Every detail in it is designed by Shakespeare from the standpoint of a self-centred prince whose only interest is in himself. First, the repeated offers of drink, which Hamlet refuses. The King begins:

Here is to thy health. Give him the cup,
says Claudius, and Hamlet:

I'll play this bout first; set it by awhile.

Then, the Queen, who obviously is meant to offer him the cup, without a word, when the audience know both that she has drunk and that the cup is poisoned:

Queen: The queen carouses to thy fortune, Hamlet.
Hamlet: Good madam!
King: Gertrude, do not drink.
Queen: I will, my lord; I pray you, pardon me.
King (aside): It is the poison'd cup: it is too late.
Hamlet: I dare not drink yet, madam; by and by.

Why these persistent refusals to offers coming from different quarters and in different circumstances? Because Shakespeare wants to emphasise the egotistic attitude of his hero by clearly separating the cause of the Queen's death and that of Hamlet's. For see what happens when the Queen dies. Shakespeare does not want his audience to believe that

Hamlet is unaware of it. The Prince, though wounded already, is the first to ask, 'How does the Queen?' Whereupon he learns that the cup was poisoned and that the Queen is dying of it. The King's responsibility is obvious. Hamlet has a weapon in his hand. But the most he can rise to is:

> Oh villany! Ho! let the door be locked.
> Treachery. Seek it out.

That he knows the King is to blame, before Laertes informs him of it, is obvious from the circumstances, but is admirably conveyed by that word 'villany', since *villain* has constantly recurred in Hamlet's vocabulary of abuse towards Claudius. Still, he does not kill.

But when Laertes reveals to him that the point of the sword was poisoned and that he is as good as dead, *he*, not merely his mother; when he sees in a flash the true motive of the King's wager, then, all procrastination is over, and he stabs the King to death.

§ 5. " *Bother !* "

An examination of Hamlet's behaviour towards the other characters in the play led us to the conclusion that the backbone of his character was a self-centredness which allowed him to take an interest in no one but his own self. Now that we have tried to discover the cause of his procrastination by examining why he killed Claudius, we are brought to the same conclusion: In the last act, Hamlet kills Claudius when Claudius attacks him. In the closet scene Hamlet thinks he kills Claudius because he thinks Claudius attacks him. Therefore, when Hamlet does not kill Claudius, i.e. throughout the whole play, the reason is that though Claudius may have killed his father he does not threaten him. This is not in Hamlet a conscious thought; it is a subconscious posture of the soul. That Claudius killed King Hamlet was an event outside Prince Hamlet's skin. It was in fact alien to him, indifferent to him. His mind was shocked by it; his emotions flowed freely beholding it; his language rose and fell like a tide at it; but that final impulse which "takes arms against a sea of troubles" and just *acts* could not be forthcoming, for the deeper Hamlet was too firmly screwed within himself ever to move outwards and give himself to any action or cause. Hamlet himself is made to express this perfectly:

The time is out of joint: O cursed spite,
That ever I was born to set it right!

These words are uttered from the bottom of his heart as the conclusion of his first meeting with the Ghost. They should be set beside his generous cry on first hearing of his father's murder:

Ghost: Murder most foul, as in the best it is;
But this most foul, strange and unnatural.
Hamlet: Haste me to know't, that I with wings as swift
As meditation or the thoughts of love,
May sweep to my revenge.

The very images which stream into his imagination to express his eagerness for revenge reveal the merely intellectual nature of this generous mood. He is, of course, sincere, bursting with sincerity. But the true measure of his deeper sincerity can be tested at once by what he does and says when he actually kills Claudius. At that moment the averred, the professed aim of the whole play, the avenging of King Hamlet's murder, comes to fruition. Hamlet does not give a thought to that. He kills Claudius because Claudius meant to kill *him*. And so he says:

Here, thou incestuous, murderous damned Dane
Drink off this potion. Is thy union here?

The abuse does conceal an allusion to his father: "murderous" after "incestuous". But that is all. The "union" is a direct allusion to Claudius' intention to poison him. I cannot see here any 'pun' about 'union' with his wife at all. If there is, it does not really matter very much. It only adds to the irrelevancy of King Hamlet at this crucial instant. Hamlet is thinking of the "pearl" which was a grain of poison for him. But neither now nor in what

remains of the play does Hamlet breathe and say: "At last,
oh father, I have avenged thee!"[1]

For, in fact, Hamlet, in spirit and intention, does not
avenge his father; he avenges himself. He had been spontaneous and sincere in assuring the Ghost that he would
"sweep to my revenge"; (notice that "my"). But he is more
sincere still a few minutes later, just after he has asked his
friends to keep the secret, has reflected on the event, and
has more coolly measured the task; for then, the distance
between his task outside and the inner core of his own true
interest, overwhelms him. "Bother!" is the mood. And it is
a musical and poetical "Bother!" which Shakespeare renders
him in the two lines:

> The time is out of joint: O cursed spite
> That ever I was born to set it right!

§ 6.   Ambition Frustrated—By Whom?

These words in which Hamlet casts his mood at the end of
the scene in which he has heard the tale of his father's
murder are of capital interest, for they express a more
general thought than the root cause of them may warrant.
Hamlet is not merely saying: "My father murdered: O
cursed spite that I was born to avenge him!" He generalises
the evil and the task. It is the whole world, "the time" as
he puts it, which is out of joint; and it is he who must set
it right.

We can perceive here the protest of the self-centred man
who, asked to perform one single task (in which he should be
interested but isn't), retorts: "Why, am I to take on every
job that needs doing in the world?" But these words are
also a resonance called forth by his father's murder from
the depth of his self-reproaching soul. Hamlet is *mentally*,
but only mentally, ambitious. At bottom, he cannot be
bothered with ambition any more than he can be bothered
with his father's death and his duty to avenge it. His later

---

[1] Steevens is, to my knowledge, the only critic who saw this point. "He kills the King at last to
revenge himself, and not his father". The Plays of W. Sh., 1778, p. 412, q. by Furness, vol. II, p. 167.

soliloquies are but meditations on the awareness that the vital passion of the spontaneous avenger was unknown to him.

Indeed, not even self-defence when the impact of danger was not too immediate. Some critics have seen a change of mood in him when he returns from his voyage to England obligingly cut short by some pirates of mercy. They read this change in his words to Horatio (V.2) after the church-yard scene:

Horatio: It must be shortly known to him from England
　　　　What is the issue of the business there.
Hamlet: It will be short; the interim is mine;
　　　　And a man's life's no more than to say "One".

This sounds most "executive" and businesslike. But Hamlet has time for just six more lines of verse when Osric calls on him. And Osric is the messenger of a King who has prepared a double barrelled plot to oust Hamlet from life while he is talking to Horatio about his regret of having forgotten himself to Laertes. The King has won again.

All this goes to show that the attitude of Hamlet for Claudius is subtler and more complex than meets the eye. The first impact is one of rights and hopes defrauded, property stolen. The King is the thief. But beneath that feeling there lurks the irritated humiliation of the powerless man at the sight of success, no matter how attained; and even an element of envy. What Hamlet feels is the defeat he had undergone when, his father dead, he let Claudius take the throne. Why did he? This question he cannot answer. He puts it to himself throughout the play; for that is what he keeps asking himself in the soliloquies under the guise of asking why he does not avenge his father. But he cannot answer.

That is the true meaning of "To be or not to be", as he himself explains in the five lines that follow. Then, mentally accepting the "not to be" branch of his dilemma, he broods on suicide, its logical conclusion; and returns to the first theme to explain his own inaction to himself as thought blasting resolution. Yet this explanation is not the right one, a fact which he half guesses as shown in his other soliloquy after he meets the Norwegian troops:

> Rightly to be great
> Is not to stir without great argument,
> But greatly to find quarrel in a straw
> When honour's at the stake.

In these soliloquies, the thought of his father is but the motive or occasion, not the essence of his cavil. What he is ever turning in his mind is his incapacity to do great things, to be great, to be. That is the question he cannot answer.

We can. Hamlet could not pour himself into action because he was too egotistic for that. All action—even crime—requires freedom from egotism. Man can only act by, so to speak, mating with the outside world; by forgetting himself for an instant, and becoming the object of his action. Hamlet could not forget himself; and, far from pouring himself into the world outside, he forced the world to pour itself into him. Since all the world was made to become Hamlet, Hamlet could neither do nor become anything in the world.

§ 7. Conclusion.

Hence his soliloquies. For, in fact, Hamlet soliloquises throughout the whole play. Whomsoever he seems to be talking to, Hamlet only speaks to Hamlet. Hence that impertinent effect of his dialogues with Rosencrantz and Guildenstern; those brusque changes and stops in what he says, with a complete indifference to the interlocutor; and that aloofness with which Hamlet seems to look down on what the other has to answer, or even on what he himself is actually saying outwards, since what matters is what he is saying inwards in an undercurrent of dialogue with himself of which his words to others are but the bubbles.

It is to this feature rather than to any deliberate imitation of insanity that the wanton twists and turns in his conversation are due. The other fellow does not matter: he is but a listening tool. This is plain in Hamlet's treatment of Polonius; but it accounts for much of his verbal behaviour towards Ophelia; as well as for those typically Hamletian phrases: "Something too much of this"; "Shall we to the court? for, by my fay, I cannot reason". "But let it be . . ." whereby he dismisses not so much the subject, which goes on beneath the surface occupying his mind, as the listening tool.

This is the inevitable outcome of his self-centredness. Just as he forces every character and every action to enter the stage of his soul, where everything happens, so he drives all the dialogues within his own thought, turning them into monologues. And it is an inexorable nemesis of this egotistic man that by dint of abolishing every human being but himself, he can talk to no one but himself.

And yet he talks. Indeed he talks much more than anyone else in the play, nearly three times as much as the King, who comes next on the list of lines spoken. Here lies the tragedy. The self-centred man gives nothing to the human beings that surround him; he wipes them out of existence so far as he is concerned—but he needs them. He needs them more anxiously perhaps than more open and generous souls would. For, by nature, the self-centred man is lonely, —inwardly lonely, and, unless he can drown this inner loneliness in outer company, he is bound to fall into misanthropy, melancholy and even madness. Hamlet was apt to feel misanthropic: "man delights not me; no, nor woman either." And his melancholy lends a sombre background to the whole play. He is ever wandering in that zone of disenchanted boredom, yet of attraction and tension towards others, to be expected of his inner contradiction—refusal to give himself to the world of men—need of the world of men.

Shakespeare has managed to convey this struggle of the two antagonistic forces right to the end. Hamlet dies in the midst of dead bodies. His mother, the King, Laertes are no more. He himself is dying. And in this solemn hour, when he might have thought of Ophelia, or of Polonius, both his victims, or of his father, at last avenged, or of his mother, poisoned, of whom, of what does he think? Of himself and of his cause. In the strongest and most moving words, he entreats Horatio to absent himself from felicity awhile "to tell my story", to "report me and my cause aright to the unsatisfied". To his dying hour, Hamlet can think of nothing but Hamlet. Both in its utter neglect of all his partners in his life and in his pathetic dependence on "the unsatisfied", this last utterance of the unhappy Prince is typical of the self-centred man.

Shakespeare could not have remained more faithful to the type which he began to draw with a firm hand from the very first scene in which he comes on the stage. There is no mystery about Hamlet. Once the film of prejudice and mis-interpretation is removed, the play stands perfectly clear; and its chief character, solidly built on sound psychological premises, is treated with all the freedom and subtle mastery of true creative genius.

CHAPTER VI

THE POET AND THE PLAY

§ 1. *The Pirate Ship.*

The study of the relations between Shakespeare and Hamlet may be approached in two ways: we may consider Shakespeare as a dramatist whose task it was to convince the greatest number of people that the few hours spent at the theatre listening to his play were agreeably passed; or we may visualise him as a great mind giving plastic dramatic expression to a subject of human interest. Our judgment of value will differ according to whether we adopt the first or the second view; and therefore it is necessary at every stage to make it clear whether we are appraising Shakespeare as an Elizabethan dramatic craftsman or as a poet of genius for all mankind and for all time.

To begin then with the narrower standard, it seems evident that even as an Elizabethan dramatic craftsman, Shakespeare blundered in overburdening his play with all the idle disquisitions about the state of the theatre in his day. True his contemporaries would be able to make more of this dialogue than a modern audience can; but no modern audience would listen with patience to a disquisition of a similar length in the midst of a moving play. The matter is wholly extraneous to the actual business in hand, and from every point of view, its inclusion must be deplored as an aesthetic blunder.

The Pyrrhus speech also holds the play for an unnecessarily long time; and for once, the audience is bound to side with Polonius when he cries out "This is too long", after listening to forty-two lines of declamatory verse. True the poet tried to break the load by allotting the first twelve lines to Hamlet, and by making Polonius provide some entertainment at this break:

> 'Fore God, my Lord, well spoken, with good accent
> and good discretion'

but there remain still thirty lines to go through, the necessity
—dramatic or aesthetic—of which is by no means plain.
The contrast between Polonius' impatience (as a garrulous
man, he objects to other persons holding forth) and Hamlet's
self-centred insistence and rude and inconsiderate retort,
is of course, an asset for the play; but the author could
equally well have brought it about much earlier. Polonius
was not impatient enough. True, also, a climax had to be
built up to bring about the player's emotion, and so lead
to Hamlet's soliloquy; but again all this need not have taken
so many words.

The pirate ship is another serious flaw in the play as a
dramatic construction. It is a weak contrivance in more
ways than one. First, in itself. Events, as wild and unruly as a
piratical attack is likely to occasion, are forced by the author
to suit his plan so well that Hamlet and only Hamlet
boarded the pirate ship and "on the instant they got clear
of our ship; so I alone became their prisoner." As if this
story was not tall enough the pirates turn out to be 'thieves
of mercy', so that the plot could go on unmolested. All this
is puerile and would not be tolerated in a modern author.

But there is worse still. Hamlet says to Horatio that this
sea fight took place the very morning after he had skilfully
stolen the King's despatch from the baggage of Rosencrantz and Guildenstern and placed the changeling instead.
It follows that Hamlet had acted thus in the expectation of
arriving in England together with the two men he was
sending "to't", since the pirates cannot have been as merci-
ful as to have given him notice of their intentions. But what
would have been the position then? The King of England
would have received a "command" from the King of Denmark to put to death two men in the suite of the Prince,
heir of Denmark, who would do what?:—profess to know
nothing about it?—know all about it? The episode simply
does not work; and everything in it goes to show that
Shakespeare did not trouble to give any likelihood to that
branch of possibility because he—though not Hamlet—

knew it would not "happen", since he had in store a ship of pirates of mercy to bring Hamlet back. By way of consequence, the whole episode disintegrates.

This piece of mechanism, despite its importance in the construction of the play, does not work. True, in the deeper movement of the emotions, the less discriminating part of the audience is not apt to notice the fact. But the excuse, valid for cheap melodrama, cannot be accepted in the case of one of the greatest dramas of all times. For the second time, but by no means the last, we have to record in Shakespeare a certain indifference to the niceties of the craft; a case we shall have to integrate together with other similar observations, not to find fault with his great play but in search of some new sidelights on the fascinating and mysterious poet behind it.

§ 2. *The Immaterial Inconsistencies.*

The many inconsistencies of detail to be found in *Hamlet* have been discussed by a number of writers and notably by the Danish critic Dr. Østerberg.[1] He rightly points out that the Elizabethan standards in these matters were not the same as ours. There are, however, limits to what a conscious artist can or cannot do; and in discussing a great artist, while of course making due allowance for the standards of his day, we must maintain the permanent standards of all art at all times. An inconsistency which does not weaken the aesthetic effect of the work does not reflect on the author; but when, through negligence or oversight, the work itself, as it was meant by the author to be, is marred, we are entitled to blame the author for a lack of harmony between design and execution.

And, to begin with, let us get rid of "inconsistencies" which only exist in the mind of the critic. Shakespeare is reproached for the fact that a local gravedigger does not recognise Hamlet, though he must have often seen the Prince; the reproach has no foundation. Those days knew

---

[1] App. III to his Essay on Hamlet's age in vol. 8 of Historisk—Filologiske Meddelelser Copenhague.

neither newspaper nor photography. It is by no means obvious that the gravedigger had ever seen Hamlet at all; and if he had, the circumstances of his arrival, his clothes, the fact that the Court was expected to turn up at the funeral from a different direction, so to speak, would justify the poet in assuming that the clown did not recognise Hamlet.

A similar observation applies to the scene of Polonius' admonition to Laertes. What does it matter that Laertes had already taken leave of his father, and that the very Polonius who urges him not to tarry, delays him with a long sermon? Is not the apparent contradiction here but a skilful stroke of the pen which adds vigour to the portrait of the garrulous old man?

There is, however, a whole set of inconsistencies of time which are real. But again, a number of them do no harm whatever to the play. King Hamlet is killed in summer, since he was asleep in the garden. His ghost comes back two months later, and, Francisco tells us "'tis bitter cold, and I am sick at heart;" nevertheless the Ghost sees the glow-worm announcing the dawn. Two months elapse again; and when Laertes returns, he finds Ophelia gathering the flowers of May and June. Finally, the lapse allowed between the first and the second arrival of Fortinbras, gives no adequate time for his campaign in Poland. This is the kind of detail no author at any time need trouble about. There is a stage-time in subtle but elastic relationship with the every day time of actually lived lives. Every playwright guesses by instinct what he can and what he cannot allow himself in this respect. In none of the cases here mentioned does Shakespeare overstep the margin set by the objective canons of his art. It is, nevertheless, useful for our purpose to point out that his tendency is rather on the side of negligence and this rather free and easy way with the facts does suggest a confidence in his powers to hoodwink his public.

§ 3. *Horatio.*

We come now to more substantial inconsistencies. The first

is that of Horatio's very character. Many are the critics who have rightly observed that Horatio does not tally with himself. In some ways, he is a stranger to the land, about which he asks obvious questions; in others, he seems to be one of the trusted courtiers of the King and Queen. He had come to the King's funeral, but does not meet Hamlet till two months later; he is a scholar who has just come from Wittenberg and yet he is the only Dane of the three on the stage who can explain the cause of Denmark's military preparations. This whom Bradley describes as "the beautiful character of Horatio"[1] is no character at all; he is but a voice Shakespeare needed to say "yes" or "no" to Hamlet or to provide information. He is in fact left behind by Hamlet as a kind of 'public relations officer' to report him and his cause aright. Far from being endowed with any "character" at all, Horatio lacks even the minimum of consistency to convince the spectators of his real existence. In this case, therefore, inconsistency does injure the artistic purpose.

Nor is it possible to follow the critics of the historical school who would consider Horatio as yet another case of a "figure" behaving in a characterless manner, now this way, now that, either as a hang-over from the sources or to suit the action. For on the one hand it is plain that the remaining "figures" do possess a consistent character; while, on the other, the patchy figure of Horatio provides an excellent example against the historical school; since it is obvious that it could easily have been endowed with perfect consistency without either unduly changing the sources or in any way impairing the action at any moment.

We are then bound to conclude that Shakespeare, who bestowed all the power of his creative genius on a character as insignificant in the play's design as Osric, did not take the trouble to melt and mould the metal of his Horatio into a living shape. Why? Does not this suggest that the actual economy of the play was not the chief controlling factor in the poet's activity?

p. 166.

§ 4. *Hamlet's Age.*

This "detail" has been left by Shakespeare in such a state of uncertainty that its discussion takes over three pages of minute print in Furness's *Variorum;* it worries Bradley and provides Østerberg with a theme for a scholarly discussion. Dr. Dover Wilson dismisses it lightly: as merely textual and of no particular importance in the theatre "since Hamlet is the age his impersonator makes him".[1] Leaving aside the fact that this latitude would allow any actor to make Hamlet older than Polonius, the view that Hamlet's age does not matter cannot be accepted. Indeed, in Østerberg's view it is the very key to the tragedy: "the clue to the tragedy of Hamlet is the sorrow of the youth or boy".

Briefly put, the problem consists in that while on the whole Hamlet gives the impression of a youth in his early twenties, the churchyard scene makes him definitely thirty. At one time or another Hamlet greets Horatio, Rosencrantz and Guildenstern as fellow-students with whom he feels in "fellowship" and in "consonancy of youth"; they have studied together at Wittenberg, and the manner of their conversation suggests youth. Hamlet is moreover the son of a woman capable of inspiring in Claudius a criminal passion. He is addicted to noting down "saws of books, forms", "pressures past" observed by youth, surely a mark of immaturity. But though he be twenty in the first three acts, he is thirty in the fifth.

Østerberg gets easily rid of the three arguments usually put forward to prove that he is thirty. The first is the word *thirty* in the first speech of the Actor-King.

> Full thirty times hath Phebus cart gone round.

This argument is worthless, and it certainly did not deserve the trouble Østerberg, and Bradley before him, took to refute it.

The second is the churchyard scene: when the clown

[1] D.W., p. 27.

113

says both that he has been sexton man and boy for thirty years and that he began to practise his craft of all days the year Hamlet was born. Here Dr. Østerberg's refutation consists in pointing out that *thirty* is one of the several stock words, such as *seven*, *twelve*, *forty*, meaning "many"; and that a clown is not a person on whom to base history or statistics.

The third is the passage about Yorick, where the clown says Yorick's skull had been in the earth for twenty-three years, while Hamlet recalls that the jester used to carry him on his back. Here again Dr. Østerberg gets rid of "twenty-three" on exactly the same grounds he used for getting rid of "thirty": it means "many" and it is a figure tossed by a clown, anyhow.

But the argument loses much of its strength by repetition. With his two stock arguments, Dr. Østerberg can refute "thirty"; and he can refute "twenty-three"; but not the combination of the two. For his refutation to be convincing it would be indispensable that the clown's "thirty" and the clown's "three and twenty" should not tally. Unfortunately for his argument, they do. It is not likely that an accumulation of figures thrown up at random by a clown would dovetail into one single result. Now here, as pointed out by Bradley,[1] we have five concrete statements, all converging on a Hamlet thirty years old.

1. The grave-digger came to his business on the day when old Hamlet defeated Fortinbras.
2. On that day young Hamlet was born.
3. The grave-digger has, at the time of speaking, been sexton for thirty years.
4. Yorick's skull has been in the earth twenty-three years.
5. Yorick used to carry young Hamlet on his back.

The accumulated effect of these five suggestions "planted" by Shakespeare in the minds of the audience is that he meant Hamlet to be thirty years old. That—whatever

[1] p. 408.

weight may be given to Dr. Østerberg's arguments—is a fact beyond dispute. Whether Shakespeare wished to produce this effect or not might be argued. But then, *on any of the two hypothesis* we have to record negligence and indifference to important issues in the play on the part of the poet; for if Dr. Østerberg is right, and Shakespeare did not mean Hamlet to be a man of thirty, but a youth of twenty (as nearly every thing else in the play would suggest) he should not have given his audience as clear and concrete an impression of "thirty" in the churchyard scene; and if Dr. Østerberg is wrong and Shakespeare did mean to convey such an impression, the chief figure in the play is now a man of thirty, now a much younger man, with unfortunate results for the work of art as such.

An examination of this problem therefore leads us to the same conclusion already established on other grounds: at times, even on important points, Shakespeare does not seem to pay much attention either to his audience or to his play.

§ *5. Hamlet and Wittenberg.*

In a note on "where was Hamlet at the time of his father's death" Dr. Bradley has lucidly examined the difficulties the text presents with regard to Hamlet's stay in Wittenberg. They start with the King's lines to him in the first act:

> For your intent
> In going back to school in Wittenberg,
> It is most retrograde to our desire.

The impression conveyed is that Hamlet came to Elsinore to attend his father's funeral. But so has Horatio, and yet Hamlet does not recognise him at once, and asks him what has brought him to Denmark. Nor is his greeting of Rosencrantz and Guildenstern, brought from Denmark precisely because the Queen is sure

> Two men there are not living
> To whom he more adheres,

such as to give the impression he has seen them recently.

The scene in which Rosencrantz and Guildenstern talk to Hamlet about the players and that in which Hamlet himself greets the players refer to a 'city' in which evidently Rosencrantz and Guildenstern live but from which Hamlet has been absent for some time. Dr. Bradley puts forward the view that Hamlet had left Wittenberg for some years. Everything then would fall into shape; for the wish to return to Wittenberg could be easily explained by the new conditions created at Elsinore by his father's death and his mother's re-marriage. This is a reasonable solution, particularly if instead of the "some years" Dr. Bradley grants, Hamlet's absence from Wittenberg is reduced to one year or even six months. The problem is therefore, *in itself*, of little importance. But it adds weight to the negligence implied in the way Hamlet's age is treated, for a thirty-year student–prince would be a somewhat strange bird at any University—let alone the fact that the ages of his three school-fellows are consequently affected.

Dr. Bradley is here led to the very conclusion to which we have so far been driven at every stage. Here are his words: "The only solution I can suggest is that, in the story or play which Shakespeare used, Hamlet and the others were all at the time of the murder young students at Wittenberg, and that, when he determined to make them older men (or to make Hamlet at any rate older), he did not take trouble enough to carry this idea through all the necessary detail, and so left some inconsistencies".

Again we come to visualise an author who does not bestow on his play or on his audience all the attention that might be expected of a good craftsman.

§ 6. *Ophelia's Death.*

When Ophelia leaves the stage after singing her pathetic songs, the King gives an order:

> *King.* Follow her close, give her good watch, I
> pray you.

Why then—it is asked—did the King's men allow her

to be drowned? This reproach is unfounded. Shakespeare must delineate his character of Claudius, positive and efficient throughout; but he need not describe in detail how or why Ophelia was able, as one "incapable of her own distress", to pass through the meshes of her watchmen and meet her fate.

The real inconsistency here is in the poetical description of her death which the Queen makes. Had this story ended with Ophelia's fall "in the weeping brook", it would have been convincing; the course of events could easily have been reconstructed by her would-be rescuers on finding her drowned, the garlands floating, the sliver broken. But that picture which follows cannot be reconciled with any constructional sense:

> Her clothes spread wide,
> And mermaid-like a while they bore her up:
> Which time she chanted snatches of old tunes,
> As one incapable of her own distress,
> Or like a creature native and indued
> Unto that element: but long it could not be
> Till that her garments, heavy with their drink,
> Pull'd the poor wretch from her melodious lay
> To muddy death.

Who saw this; and worst of all, who *heard* this scene and let the "poor wretch" be drowned? This scene is one of the worst examples of negligence and indifference towards the true construction of the play and of lack of respect for his audience to be found in Shakespeare.

It is saved by the sheer magic of poetical imagination which went to its making and pervades it throughout. Charmed off into a world of dreams, the audience forget all about construction and logic. The analyst, coldly holding a *post-mortem* after the lights of poetry are out, is inclined to suspect a sinister logic beneath it all. He remembers the cold reaction of the Queen on being told that Ophelia was at her door. "I will not speak with her", had she said to an unspoken request. And when Horatio, working on

her fears and on no other more human or compassionate
feeling, succeeds in altering her decision, all she says is
"Let her come in". The Queen loathes the very thought of
Ophelia. She feels Ophelia is the living witness of all the
disasters her own behaviour is piling over the two unfortunate families. So, when she tells how Ophelia died,
so leisurely, with so much detail, the suspicion arises that
she saw and heard it all and budged not, that this pathetic
token and victim of her own folly should vanish out of her
and everybody's sight.

Was this Shakespeare's intention? If so, the Queen's
poetic speech would regain some logic, though it would still
be open to criticism; for the Queen would then be giving
herself away. In any case, and on whatever ground we chose
to stand, Shakespeare is again here indifferent to the inner
logic of the play and somewhat contemptuous of his
audience.

§ 7.   Shakespeare's Aloofness.

This conclusion is now becoming something of a leitmotiv.
A number of examples have led us to discover that the poet
who wrote *Hamlet* did not seem always to take his play
as much in earnest as we do; nor his public either. Hamlet's
remark about the "excellent play" which was "caviare to
the general" and "pleased not the million" certainly echoes
the attitude of Shakespeare to his public; and so does
Hamlet's rude remark to the player on Polonius: "he's for
a jig or a tale of bawdry, or he sleeps".

We must therefore see in Shakespeare a man of exceptional gifts as a *poet* in the deepest sense of this word, a
man, that is, endowed with the gift of seeing at a glance
the general picture and the details of human nature and of
re-creating it all through his power over words; but also a
man who through some "truant disposition", some anarchical
indiscipline, the very superabundance of his gifts, which he
seems at times unable to canalise, or possibly owing to the
very greatness of his mind, and also to some kink or defect

in his character, did not always *serve* his genius with the devotion such divine gifts require; so that he often remains below, beside, at times above his work, curiously unable or unwilling to throw himself unreservedly into it and become one with it.

This attitude of the poet towards his work explains the inconsistencies already observed, whether of the kind that matter and impair his creation or of the kind that do not so. It accounts also for the unwieldy nature of some of his plays, such as *King Lear* and this very *Hamlet*, a magnificent dramatic poem, but a defective—or should we say excessive —play since it cannot be staged as Shakespeare wrote it. In this sense, Shakespeare was above his theatre, certainly above *Hamlet*; for his dramatic poem is played daily in the minds of well-read men all over the world, on a mental stage, far surpassing the stage for which it was written.

§ 8. *Puns and Quibbles.*

Puns are often in Shakespeare releases for his imagination to "gambol" from the tracks of thought. More often than not he controls them; at times they come precious near to controlling him. When the scene, and above all the character, allow it or lend themselves to it, Shakespeare is in his element. Polonius is a godsend for him. By lending Hamlet an antic disposition, he can also release many a pun that comes to his imagination. The very first line Hamlet has to say in the play contains, is in fact, a play upon words:

A little more than kin and less than kind

and the second, his answer to the King, comes as near a a pun as it can without actually being one.

Not so, my lord; I am too much i'the sun.

Three lines earlier, the King has said:

But now, my cousin Hamlet, and my son—

A distinguished editor of *Hamlet* goes as far as to print *son* instead of *sun* in this line of Hamlet. But this would appear to rest on a mistaken view of what a pun is. For a pun to exist, the phrase must have a meaning—if not necessarily the same meaning—whichever way it is written. Now "I am too much i'the son" has no meaning; even if we can guess what Hamlet might have meant by it. The point has its importance because this is a good example of the way Shakespeare's imagination often works.[1] Shakespeare does not merely make his thought leap from meaning to meaning by actual definite puns—a method he follows often enough—but also by what might be described as mental resonances or hints at a pun actually not developed or used. This case sun-son is typical.

But we have an even better example in Hamlet's scene with Osric. This "water-fly" has just extolled Laertes in an extravagant language, as "an absolute gentleman, full of most excellent differences, of very soft society and great showing; indeed, to speak feelingly of him, he is the card or calendar of gentry, for you shall find in him the continent of what part a gentleman would see". Osric has excelled himself, and he ends with a fine show of incoherent fireworks. But Hamlet answers in perfect gibberish, and he handles nonsense so successfully that some critics have solemnly wondered whether the text might not be corrupt. Yet there is method in the way Shakespeare pours forth this madness: "Sir, his definement suffers no perdition in you; though I know to divide him inventorially would dizzy the arithmetic of memory and yet but yaw neither, in respect of his quick sail. But, in the verity of extolment, I take him to be a soul of great article, and his infusion of such dearth and rareness, as to make true diction of him, his semblable in his mirror, and who else would trace him, his umbrage, nothing more". The passage is full of mental resonances, not quite puns, but hints at possible ones: "article" hinting at "inventory", "divide" at "part" used by Osric; "yaw" and "sail" at Osric's "card and calendar"; "sail" again at "sale", "article" and "inventory".

Yet it is patent that in this as in many other cases in the play, where verbal quibbling becomes riotous, the audience

[1] No one has shown this better than Dr. Dover Wilson.

cannot catch the subtle verbal effects which at the time of writing are tickling the poet's mind. We are here, again, in the presence of a great mind so richly endowed that he bursts the framework of his own creations; a genius who, though as conscious in his work as any artist ever was, is often betrayed out of his set purpose by the volcanic force of his creative impulses. This feature of Shakespeare's work leads us to a somewhat curious parallel between the poet and his protagonist. Like Hamlet, Shakespeare is at times speaking to no one but himself. The audience are a pretext for him to speak aloud. Many of the subtle things he utters are for his own exclusive consumption. To a considerable extent, *Hamlet* is a soliloquy addressed by Shakespeare to Shakespeare.

§ 9. *Shakespeare's Comic Sense.*

There is one aspect—so far unnoticed—of Shakespeare's attitude to his play, in which his "truant disposition" injures his aesthetic conception as a whole. I refer to his irrepressible comic sense. The comic sense of the poet who created Falstaff was bound to be robust and riotous, and therefore, apt to burst out even at times and in places where it was not required. We may be now able to understand this oddity in Shakespeare's work, having already come to the conclusion that *Hamlet* is in a sense a soliloquy spoken by Shakespeare without too much consideration for his audience.

Thus, Shakespeare will not hesitate to set down a phrase which tickles his sense of humour even though it does not suit the objective situation. Fun to him, though not fun to the public, in it goes. We can see him at his desk imagining an amusing line or two, fully realising that they are not justified by the situation, yet writing them down just because he cannot resist it, and because he does not respect his audience and feels they will swallow anything anyhow.

No other explanation is possible, for instance, for the second of these two lines:

King. Thanks, Rosencrantz and gentle
 Guildenstern.
Queen. Thanks, Guildenstern and gentle
 Rosencrantz.

Of course, "gentle" was needed for scanning the lines;
of course, the Queen might wish to make Guildenstern feel
as important as Rosencrantz; the fact remains that, Shakespeare being Shakespeare, he could not fail to see how
incongruously comic the inverted repetition was bound to
be. He therefore wrote these two lines either in spite or
because of their comic effect; and as the first conclusion is
to be excluded in the case of such an artist, it follows that
he wrote the Queen's line (quite unnecessary by the way)
because it tickled his fancy as "absolute fun", though in its
context it is not fun at all and mars the passage.

This surmise is strengthened by the scrutiny of other
passages which show Shakespeare poking fun not merely at
words but at his audience. Here is a case in point. The
King's first speech makes Shakespeare concentrate on the
state of mind of a man placed between a funeral and a
wedding. His sense of fun, along with his general trend to
philosophize, which he shares with Hamlet, draws him away
from psychology to abstraction, and so he writes, and makes
the King say these lines:

Therefore our sometime sister, now our queen (. . .)
Have we, as 'twere with a defeated joy,
With one auspicious and one dropping eye,
With mirth in funeral and with dirge in marriage,
In equal scale weighing delight and dole,
Taken to wife.

Obviously, this is not what such a king at such a
moment should say. Shakespeare himself, beholding the
sight from above the play, struck by its balance and poise
between joy and grief, writes those see-saw lines, thoroughly
amused by *them*, and not caring a rap for—or forgetting—
the likelihood of it all.

What was Shakespeare's own attitude towards the Ghost?

Is it and must it remain as "secret" as some of his students assert?[1] The cellarage scene has been explained as a stratagem to put Marcellus off the scent; for he must not know that the Ghost was actually King Hamlet's spirit; and so Hamlet, in a spontaneous conspiracy with the Ghost, does all he can to make Marcellus for good and Horatio temporarily believe that the apparition is a devil come from hell.[2] But why should Marcellus be kept in the dark as to the "honesty" of the Ghost? For fear of an indiscretion? Then, why the oath? And what could he reveal since he had not heard what the Ghost had said? This explanation is far too subtle and carries no conviction.

Shakespeare's own attitude towards the Ghost is no mystery. About ghosts in general he was a sceptic with an open mind—just as Horatio before the actual apparition convinced him. The proof of this view is the way in which he makes the four witnesses react to the vision each in his own manner; which shows that he, Shakespeare, was free, not only from belief but from disbelief as well. But about the particular Ghost in *Hamlet*, Shakespeare's opinion was that it was an excellent piece of dramatic mechanism which had to impress his audience by its "reality", but which could not impress the author at all, since he was making it up.

His problem, therefore, was to make his audience believe in his Ghost even though he did not believe in it himself. He went about it ably enough, for his dramatic skill was unrivalled, provided he took trouble enough and was not betrayed by his buoyant spirits into some antic. And sure enough the Ghost becomes real even before it has spoken, thanks to the consummate skill lavished on its first two visitations and on the talk before and after, on the platform.

Things, however, begin to go awry precisely at the most solemn moment. The dialogue between Hamlet and his father's spirit has just begun when a whiff of flippancy and

[1] See, for instance, D.W., p. 85.

[2] See D.W., p. 79, ss.

fun passes through Shakespeare's mind. It is irrepressible.
And so, in the midst of the utmost solemnity, incongruous
humour bursts forth—a humour which is not in the
characters, but in the poet behind them.

> *Ghost:*   My hour is almost come,
> When I to sulphurous and tormenting flames
> Must render up myself.
>
> *Hamlet:*   Alas, poor ghost!

This is Shakespeare laughing with Shakespeare through
Hamlet, just as Hamlet, in the play, laughs with Hamlet
through Polonius. True it might be interpreted as a Protestant hint at the crowd on the laughability of the belief in
Purgatory; and those who attach a particular importance to
the differences between Protestants and Catholics on the
subject of ghosts might have availed themselves of this
detail. This view, however, requires that Hamlet II should
be protestant and Hamlet I catholic; and it puts too nice a
distinction on Shakespeare's words. In what concerns this
particular episode, Hamlet's "Alas, poor Ghost!" can have
no such theological background or intention, for a second
quiet chuckle comes from the poet to warn us that he is not
really poking fun at Catholic theology, but at the Ghost
itself.

> *Ghost:* Pity me not, but lend thy serious hearing
> To what I shall unfold.

To which Hamlet makes this truly comic answer:

> Speak: I am bound to hear.

Aloof from his work, contemptuous of his audience,
Shakespeare laughs under his sleeve at all this mummery he
puts in operation to start his play. He is both in and out
of it. He constructs his ghost scenes with the utmost skill, but
now and then he is overpowered by a "truant disposition",
and, at the risk of impairing his work, he smiles or even
laughs at the most solemn moments. He laughs because he
can imagine the audience taken in by his story; and then
he makes his Ghost say with his cavernous voice things no
man could read without laughing outright:

> But that I am forbid
> To tell the secrets of my prison-house,
> I could a tale unfold whose lightest word
> Would harrow thy soul, freeze thy young blood,
> Make thy two eyes, like stars, start from their
>   spheres,
> Thy knotted and combined locks to part
> And each particular hair to stand an end,
> Like quills upon the fretful porpentine;

It is utterly impossible to accept these lines as what Shakespeare really thought the situation objectively required. He wrote them deliberately, because his inner comic devil got the better of him; because as a genius endowed with an overwhelming sense of fun he was irrepressible, and because the very idea of the Ghost made him merry.

The same mood of flippant mirth overpowers Shakespeare when he makes the Ghost appear again during the bedroom scene. It is, however, a subtler mood. The humorous surge this time does not fully succeed in overcoming the earnest attitude of the poet; nevertheless, a playful smile can be caught fleeting across his face as he writes the lines the Queen addresses her son:

> Alas, how is't with you,
> That you do bend your eye on vacancy
> And with the incorporal air do hold discourse?
> Forth at your eyes your spirits wildly peep;
> And, as the sleeping soldiers in the alarm,
> Your bedded hair, like life in excrements,
> Starts up and stands an end.

The very subtlety of the mood in this passage helps us to realise how the other similar passage in the first speech of the Ghost to Hamlet could have come to be written. For, of course, even in that first passage the grave mood prevails. In general and normally, Shakespeare treats the Ghost with earnestness and respect; after all, such is the mood in which he wants it treated by his audience. But now and then, he strays out of the world of illusion he has so skilfully created, sees the fun of it, and mischievously sets down in a line or two of comic verse the smile it raises in him.

His audience? Why, they would lap it up and be impressed. And such is the mood in which he must also have written the cellarage scene. Here we come upon one of those cases when the mood of the character and situation calls forth a resonance in the natural tendencies of the author. Such a case occurred when Polonius, provoked by Ophelia, breaks out into a cascade of puns on the word "tenders", much to the delight of the pun-loving author. Here again, in the cellarage scene, Hamlet feels somewhat unhinged by what he has just experienced, and so he must behave in an irresponsible way, instinctively trying, so to speak, to regain some balance by spreading sails to the winds of nonsense on feeling buffeted by such deep seas. This enables Shakespeare to regale the general public with a scene of coarse fun cum supernatural terror. The idea that the Ghost bellows "Swear!" from "the cellarage" in order to hoodwink an inconvenient witness is over-subtle. All we have is an author with an irrepressible sense of fun, a simple and somewhat coarse public, and a situation lending itself to an enjoyable combination of comic and terrific effects, nicely shared out by Shakespeare in different doses: for the "general" who will swallow everything, and for the judicious, who will quietly smile and understand.

§ 10.   Caviare To The General.

This contempt of Shakespeare for his public is writ large in some of his puns. For instance:

Pol.: I did enact Julius Caesar; I was killed i'the Capitol; Brutus killed me.

Ham.: It was a brute part of him to kill so capital a calf there.

Who can believe that Shakespeare was not aware of the value of this kind of humour? The two puns of Hamlet's answer are so laboriously prepared, with that "Brutus killed me" as a kind of afterthought for the groundlings who might not know enough Roman history, that Shakespeare's fusing inspiration and improvisation cannot be here adduced in extenuation of this outburst of downright bad taste as they can in the case of Ophelia's "tenders". No. Here Shakespeare is sinning against the sentiment he makes Hamlet express in the Prince's observation to the player that this kind of thing "though it make the unskilful laugh, cannot but make the judicious grieve."

Hamlet shows but too many signs of this contempt in which Shakespeare held his audiences. A certain lack of measure, a bombast, an exaggeration, comes now and then to remind the fastidious reader that the author was only too ready to pander to the worst tastes of the crowd. How else are we to explain the beginning of the soliloquy at the close of Act III scene II:

> 'Tis now the very witching time of night,
> When churchyards yawn, and hell itself breathes out
> Contagion to this world; now could I drink hot
> blood,
> And do such bitter business as the day
> Would quake to look on.

No one in his senses can maintain that Shakespeare did not realise that he was writing sheer nonsense in these lines and marring the style and figure of the Prince for the judicious. Here is, again, what Shakespeare makes Laertes say on hearing Ophelia is drowned:

> Too much of water hast thou, poor Ophelia,
> And therefore I forbid my tears.

Shakespeare was bound to know this was poor stuff. It is by no means consonant with the character of Laertes, a hot-blooded youth with no particular gift for such metaphors and complexities; it can stand here as nothing but an appeal to maudlin sentimentality.

And what are we to think of the scene in the graveyard between the two young bloods? When all has been said about the necessity of showing Hamlet here ranting as well as Laertes, this page cannot be read without some literary repugnance. Given the characters and the situation, the unseemly squabble by or even in Ophelia's grave is plausible. But the wording of it! The extravagant nonsense Hamlet utters cannot be excused even on grounds of madness, real or simulated. But any such excuse is out of the question for Laertes, and yet he is made to say:

> Hold off the earth awhile,
> Till I have caught her once more in mine arms.
> Now pile your dust upon the quick and dead,
> Till of this flat a mountain you have made
> To o'er-top old Pelion or the skyish head
> Of blue Olympus.

Here again Shakespeare was bound to know that he was writing stuff and nonsense; and therefore the only possible explanation is that he knew the public liked it. He evidently agreed with his contemporary Lope de Vega:

> Since the groundlings are all foolish
> And since it is they who pay,
> We must talk to them in foolish
> So they can enjoy the play.[1]

§ 11.   *The Poet and The Prince.*

The criticisms here offered refer to one of the masterpieces of all times and to the greatest of European poets. They should be read with due reference to the outstanding quality of the author and the play. Indeed, it is because of this very excellence that the blemishes pointed out above strike the mind even as a scratch on a surface of polished gold offends the eye more vividly than on a less noble metal.

The purpose of these observations is to endeavour to contribute to the understanding of both *Hamlet* and Shakespeare, by pointing out how even the abundance of his gifts works at times against the poet. This is the case, in particular with the havoc Shakespeare's astonishing imagination some-

[1] El vulgo es necio y, pues que paga, es justo
Hablarle en necio para darle gusto.

times plays with his style. The speed of his creation is so overpowering that images overtop images in succeeding waves, so that it often happens that five or six lines, through sheer density, become opaque without becoming dark— very much like the white foam of a precipitous torrent which, though itself luminous, allows no light through; while in other passages his thought struggles desperately for freedom, entangled in coils within coils of words and phrases, like a Laocoon.

Impatience. And, again, that enigmatic, grave, even sad but smiling and at times laughing face of the *grand seigneur des lettres* Shakespeare must have been; heir to a kingdom of mediaeval ghosts, murderers and revengers, watching the rising surge of the groundlings and of the "baser sort"; piercing with unfailing eyes the innermost sinews of human behaviour, struck now by the pity of it, now by the fun of it, and in either case feeling himself very much out of it; *mentally* in sympathy, in unity perhaps, with all that pageantry which turns into a river of colour the paltry tale told by an idiot that human history really is; at heart, however, distant and aloof, unable to pour himself out into that life there and lose his own life in it so as to gain his soul; a keen light, a cold flame, no smoke; and down there at the very root of his being, the void, the disappointment and the frustration of a life lived only in the reflected image of a mirror, of one of the greatest minds the world ever knew—yet, for all that, a mere image of a life, not life itself. And this void, this disappointment and this frustration of Shakespeare are perhaps the dimensions in depth which add so much gravity, sonority, resonance to the lightest vibration in his poetry, and make of Shakespeare the Hamlet of Parnassus and of Hamlet the Shakespeare of the stage.

BIBLIOGRAPHY

BRADLEY   *Shakespearean Tragedy.*
Lectures on Hamlet, Othello, King Lear, Macbeth.
By A. C. Bradley, London, 1904.

CAIRNCROSS   *The Problem of Hamlet.*
A Solution by A. S. Cairncross, London, 1936.

D.W.   *What Happens in Hamlet.*
By J. Dover Wilson, Cambridge, 1935.

D.W.H.   *The Works of Shakespeare.*
Edited for the Syndics of the Cambridge University Press
by John Dover Wilson.
The Tragedy of Hamlet, Prince of Denmark.
Cambridge, 1934.

D.W.M.   *The Manuscript of Shakespeare's* Hamlet *and the Problems of
its Transmission.*
By J. Dover Wilson, Cambridge, 1934.

DOWDEN   *The Works of Shakespeare.*
The Tragedy of Hamlet.
Edited by Edward Dowden, London, 1933.

E.E.S.   *Elizabeth and Essex.*
A Tragic History by Lytton Strachey, London, 1928.

FURNESS   *Shakspere (William).*
A new Variorum edition of Shakespeare edited by H. H.
Furness, Philadelphia and London, 1871–95, vols. 3 and 4,
1877.

ØSTERBERG   *Prince Hamlet's Age.*
By V. Østerberg, København, 1924.
Det Kgl. Danske Videnskaberner Selsbab Historisk-filologiske
Meddelelser VIII 4.

SCHÜCKING   *Die Charakterprobleme bei Shakespeare.*
Von Levin L. Schücking, Leipzig, 1927.

STOLL–A.   *Art and Artifice in Shakespeare.*
By Elmer Edgar Stoll, Cambridge, 1933.

STOLL–H.   *Shakespeare Studies Historical and Comparative in Method.*
By Elmer Edgar Stoll, New York, 1927.